SEVENTH-DAY ADVENTIST® | CHURCH MANUAL

SEVENTH-DAY ADVENTIST® | **CHURCH MANUAL**

**19TH EDITION
REVISED 2015**

Published by the Secretariat
General Conference of Seventh-day Adventists®

Published by the Review & Herald Publishing Association.

Printed in U.S.A.

15 14 13 12 11   5 4 3 2 1

ISBN   978-0-8280-2821-9   hardcover
ISBN   978-0-8280-2820-2   paperback

Printed and distributed by the
Pacific Press® Publishing Association
Nampa, Idaho 83653-5353

Table of Contents

CHAPTER 1

Why a *Church Manual*?

Why does the Seventh-day Adventist Church have a *Church Manual*? God is a God of order as evidenced in His works of creation and redemption. Consequently, order belongs to the essence of His church. Order is achieved through principles and regulations that guide the Church in its internal operations and in the fulfillment of its mission to the world. In order for it to be a successful ecclesiastical organization at the service of the Lord and humanity, it needs order, rule, and discipline. Scripture affirms that "all things be done decently and in order" (1 Cor. 14:40).

Ellen G. White pointed out such needs in 1875: "The church of Christ is in constant peril. Satan is seeking to destroy the people of God, and one man's mind, one man's judgment, is not sufficient to be trusted. Christ would have His followers brought together in church capacity, observing order, having rules and discipline, and all subject one to another, esteeming others better than themselves."—3T 445.

But Church leaders did not quickly produce a book of rules for Church governance, even though the General Conference Session met annually during the Church's early years and delegates voted on matters of church order and life. Finally, in 1882, the General Conference Session voted to have prepared "instructions to church officers, to be printed in the *Review and Herald* or in tract form."—RH, Dec. 26, 1882. This revealed the growing realization that order was imperative if organization was to function effectively and that uniformity in order required its guiding principles to be put into printed form.

However, when the proposal to place the articles in permanent form as a church manual came before the 1883 General Conference Session, delegates rejected the idea. They feared a manual might formalize the Church and take from its pastors their individual freedom to deal with matters of order as they desired.

But this fear—doubtless reflecting the opposition that had existed 20 years before to any kind of organization—evidently soon lessened. The annual General Conference Sessions continued to take actions on matters of order.

Though the Church officially declined to adopt a manual, leaders from time to time gathered together in book or booklet-form the generally accepted rules of church life. Perhaps the most impressive was a 184-page book published in 1907 by pioneer J. N. Loughborough entitled

The Church, Its Organization, Order and Discipline, which dealt with many of the topics now covered by this *Church Manual*.

As the Church worldwide grew rapidly in the early twentieth century, it increasingly recognized the need for a manual for worldwide use by its pastors and lay members. In 1931 the General Conference Committee voted to publish a church manual. J. L. McElhany, later president of the General Conference, prepared the manuscript, which was published in 1932.

The opening sentence of the preface of that first edition observed that "it has become increasingly evident that a manual on church government is needed to set forth and preserve our denominational practices and polity."

Note the word *preserve*. This was no attempt to suddenly create and impose upon the Church a whole pattern of church governance. Rather it was an endeavor first to *preserve* all the good actions taken through the years and then to add rules required by the Church's increasing growth and complexity.

Authority and Function of the *Church Manual*

The *Church Manual* has existed in its current format since 1932. It describes the operation and functions of local churches and their relationship to denominational structures in which they hold membership. The *Church Manual* also expresses the Church's understanding of Christian life and church governance and discipline based on biblical principles and the authority of duly assembled General Conference Sessions. "God has ordained that the representatives of His church from all parts of the earth, when assembled in a General Conference, shall have authority."—9T 261.

The *Church Manual* is divided into two types of material. The content of each chapter is of worldwide value and is applicable to every church organization, congregation, and member. Recognizing the need for variations in some sections, additional explanatory material, presented as guidance and examples, appears as notes at the end of the *Church Manual*. The notes have subheadings corresponding to chapter subheadings and page numbers of the main text.

The standards and practices of the Church are based upon the principles of the Holy Scriptures. These principles, underscored by the Spirit of Prophecy, are set forth in this *Church Manual*. They are to be followed in all matters pertaining to the administration and operation of local churches. The *Church Manual* also defines the relationship that exists between the local congregation and the conference or other entities of Seventh-day Adventist denominational organization. No attempt should be made to set up standards of membership or to make, or attempt to enforce, rules or regulations for local church operations that are contrary to these decisions adopted by the General Conference in Session and that are set forth in this *Church Manual.*

Making Changes

The General Conference through the years voted important changes concerning the *Church Manual.* Realizing the importance of conducting the worldwide work of the Church "decently and in order," the 1946 General Conference Session voted that "all changes or revisions of policy that are to be made in the Manual shall be authorized by the General Conference Session."—*General Conference Report*, No. 8, p. 197 (June 14, 1946).

In 1948, recognizing that local conditions sometimes call for special actions, the General Conference Committee voted that "each division, including the North American Division of the world field, prepare a 'Supplement' to the new *Church Manual* not in any way modifying it but containing such additional matter as is applicable to the conditions and circumstances prevailing in the division; the manuscripts for these Supplements to be submitted to the General Conference Committee for endorsement before being printed."—*Autumn Council Actions*, 1948, p. 19.

The 2000 General Conference Session authorized the reclassification of some existing *Church Manual* material into the Notes section as guidance and examples rather than mandatory material, and approved the process for making changes. Changes in the *Church Manual*, except for the notes and editorial changes, can be made only by action of a General Conference Session, where delegates of the world church have voice and vote. If a local church, conference, or union conference/mission wishes to propose a *Church Manual* revision, it should submit its proposal to the next constituent level for counsel and study. If that level approves the proposal, it submits the suggested revision to the next level for additional evaluation. If the various levels approve the proposal, it eventually comes before the General Conference *Church Manual* Committee, which considers all recommendations. If the *Church Manual* Committee approves a revision, it prepares it for presentation at an Annual Council and/or General Conference Session.

Revision of a note follows the same procedure. The General Conference Executive Committee may approve changes to the notes at any Annual Council.

The *Church Manual* Committee reports proposed nonsubstantive editorial changes to the main content of the *Church Manual* to an Annual

Council of the General Conference Executive Committee, which may give final approval. However, in the event the Annual Council determines by one-third vote that an editorial change substantively alters the meaning of a passage, the proposed change must go to the General Conference Session.

At the final Annual Council of a quinquennium, the General Conference Executive Committee reviews all changes to the notes and coordinates the changes with any proposed amendments to the main content of the *Church Manual*.

A new edition of the *Church Manual* is published after every General Conference Session. The most recent edition should always be used. This edition incorporates amendments made at the 2015 General Conference Session.

Where to Get Advice

Church officers and leaders, pastors, and members should consult with their conference for advice pertaining to the operating of their congregation or on questions arising from the *Church Manual*. If they do not reach mutual understanding, they should consult with their union conference/mission for clarification.

Terms Used in the *Church Manual*

Church—For editorial and printing economy, "Church," with a capital C, in these pages is used in place of the full term "Seventh-day Adventist Church" and refers to the overall Church organization rather than to a local church or congregation, with the exception of when it is referred to within a quotation.

Conference, mission, section, delegation, field, union of churches—For purposes of editorial and printing economy, "conference" in these pages means "conference, mission, field, section, delegation, or union of churches," as the administrative context indicates. Generally, each congregation is a member of the sisterhood of churches known as a conference, but until the local organization achieves conference status, under General Conference *Working Policy* it may be identified as a mission, section, delegation, or field. In some world divisions, unions of churches in a particular country function as a conference for local-church purposes and as a union for other Church organizational purposes. (See Chapter 3, "Organization and Authority.")

Pastor and minister—Most areas of the world Church use "pastor" to identify a member of the clergy, so that term is used in these pages rather than "minister," regardless of the responsibilities assigned by the local conference. Use of the term here is not intended to mandate that usage where the custom is to use "minister." Pastors referred to in this manual are those who have been appointed by the conference to oversee the affairs of the local church or district.

Abbreviations of Ellen G. White's books are identified on p. 186.

Scripture quotations are taken from the New King James Version unless otherwise indicated, with the exception of when referred to within a Spirit of Prophecy quotation.

CHAPTER 2

Church of the Living God

Scripture uses various expressions to describe the church, such as "the church of God" (Acts 20:28), "the body of Christ" (Eph. 4:12), and "the church of the living God" (1 Tim. 3:15).

To belong to the church of God is a unique and soul-satisfying privilege. It is God's purpose to gather out a people from the far corners of the earth to bind them into one body, the body of Christ, of which He is the living head. All who are children of God in Christ Jesus are members of this body, and in this relationship they may enjoy fellowship with each other and fellowship also with their Lord.

The Bible uses the word *church* in at least two senses: a general sense applying to the church in all the world (Matt. 16:18; 1 Cor. 12:28) and a particular sense applying to the church in a city or a province, such as to those at Rome (Rom. 1:6, 7), Corinth (1 Cor. 1:2), and Thessalonica (1 Thess. 1:1) and of Galatia (1 Cor. 16:1), Asia (1 Cor. 16:19), and Syria and Cilicia (Acts 15:41).

Christ, being the head of the church and its living Lord, has a deep love for the members of His body. In the church He is to be glorified (Eph. 3:21). Through the church He will reveal the "manifold wisdom of God" (Eph. 3:10). Day by day He nourishes the church (Eph. 5:29), and His longing desire is to make of it "a glorious church, not having spot or wrinkle or any such thing, but that she should be holy and without blemish" (Eph. 5:27).

No Wall of Partition

Christ sought by precept and example to teach the truth that with God there was to be no dividing wall between Israel and other nations (John 4:4-42; 10:16; Luke 9:51-56; Matt. 15:21-28). The apostle Paul writes, "The Gentiles should be fellow heirs, of the same body, and partakers of His promise in Christ through the gospel" (Eph. 3:6).

Nor is there to be among Christ's followers any preference of caste or nationality or race or color, for all are of one blood. The elect of God are a universal brotherhood, a new humanity, "all one in Christ Jesus" (Gal. 3:28).

"Christ came to this earth with a message of mercy and forgiveness. He laid the foundation for a religion by which Jew and Gentile, black and white, free and bond, are linked together in one common brotherhood, recognized as equal in the sight of God. The Savior has a boundless love for every human being."—7T 225.

"No distinction on account of nationality, race, or caste is recognized by God. He is the Maker of all mankind. All men are of one family by creation, and all are one through redemption. Christ came to demolish every wall of partition, to throw open every compartment of the temple, that every soul may have free access to God. . . . In Christ there is neither Jew nor Greek, bond nor free. All are brought nigh by His precious blood."— COL 386.

Supreme Object of Christ's Regard

Those in Christ's service who are called to leadership are to "take care of the church" (1 Tim. 3:5), to "shepherd the church of God" (Acts 20:28), and to show "concern for all the churches" (2 Cor. 11:28).

"I testify to my brethren and sisters that the church of Christ, enfeebled and defective as it may be, is the only object on earth on which He bestows His supreme regard. While He extends to all the world His invitation to come to Him and be saved, He commissions His angels to render divine help to every soul that cometh to Him in repentance and contrition, and He comes personally by His Holy Spirit into the midst of His church."— TM 15.

As the bride of Christ and the supreme object of His regard, the church is expected in all its functions to represent the order and the character of the divine.

"At this time the church is to put on her beautiful garments—'Christ our righteousness.' There are clear, decided distinctions to be restored and exemplified to the world in holding aloft the commandments of God and the faith of Jesus. The beauty of holiness is to appear in its native luster in contrast with the deformity and darkness of the disloyal, those who have revolted from the law of God. Thus we acknowledge God, and recognize His law, the foundation of His government in heaven and throughout His earthly dominions. His authority should be kept distinct and plain before the world, and no laws are to be acknowledged that come in collision with the laws of Jehovah. If in defiance of God's arrangements the world be allowed to influence our decisions or our actions, the purpose of God is defeated. However specious the pretext, if the church waver here, there is written against her in the books of heaven a betrayal of the most sacred trusts, and treachery to the kingdom of Christ. The church is firmly and decidedly to hold her principles before the whole heavenly universe and the kingdoms of the world; steadfast fidelity in maintaining the honor and sacredness of the law of God will attract the notice and admiration of even the world, and many will, by the good works which they shall behold, be led to glorify our Father in heaven."—TM 16, 17.

The apostle Peter writes, "But you are a chosen generation, a royal priesthood, a holy nation, His own special people, that you may proclaim the praises of Him who called you out of darkness into His marvelous light" (1 Peter 2:9).

Complete in Christ

"The Lord has provided His church with capabilities and blessings, that they may present to the world an image of His own sufficiency, and that His church may be complete in Him, a continual representation of another, even the eternal world, of laws that are higher than earthly laws. His church is to be a temple built after the divine similitude, and the angelic architect has brought his golden measuring rod from heaven, that every stone may be hewed and squared by the divine measurement and polished to shine as an emblem of heaven, radiating in all directions the bright, clear beams of the Sun of Righteousness. . . .

"The Lord Jesus is making experiments on human hearts through the exhibition of His mercy and abundant grace. He is effecting transformations so amazing that Satan, with all his triumphant boasting, with all his confederacy of evil united against God and the laws of His government, stands viewing them as a fortress impregnable to his sophistries and delusions. They are to him an incomprehensible mystery. The angels of God, seraphim and cherubim, the powers commissioned to cooperate with human agencies, look on with astonishment and joy that fallen men, once children of wrath, are through the training of Christ developing characters after the divine similitude, to be sons and daughters of God, to act an important part in the occupations and pleasures of heaven.

"To His church, Christ has given ample facilities, that He may receive a large revenue of glory from His redeemed, purchased possession. The church, being endowed with the righteousness of Christ, is His depository, in which the wealth of His mercy, His love, His grace, is to appear in full and final display. . . .

"In their untainted purity and spotless perfection, Christ looks upon His people as the reward of all His suffering, His humiliation, and His love, and the supplement of His glory—Christ, the great center from which radiates all glory. 'Blessed are they which are called unto the marriage supper of the Lamb.' "—TM 17-19.

The church is committed to the foregoing principles of the spiritual unity of Christ's church. By the peace and power which Christ's righteousness brings, the church pledges to conquer every barrier that sin has erected between human beings.

CHAPTER 3

Organization and Authority

Church organization is based on God's principles. "Never allow anyone's ideas to unsettle your faith in regard to the order and harmony which should exist in the church. . . . The God of heaven is a God of order, and He requires all His followers to have rules and regulations, and to preserve order."—5T 274.

Biblical Basis for Organization

When God called the children of Israel out of Egypt and chose them as His peculiar people, He provided for them an impressive system of organization to govern their conduct in both civil and religious matters.

"The government of Israel was characterized by the most thorough organization, wonderful alike for its completeness and its simplicity. The order so strikingly displayed in the perfection and arrangement of all God's created works was manifest in the Hebrew economy. God was the center of authority and government, the sovereign of Israel. Moses stood as their visible leader, by God's appointment, to administer the laws in His name. From the elders of the tribes a council of seventy was afterward chosen to assist Moses in the general affairs of the nation. Next came the priests, who consulted the Lord in the sanctuary. Chiefs, or princes, ruled over the tribes. Under these were 'captains over thousands, and captains over hundreds, and captains over fifties, and captains over tens,' and, lastly, officers who might be employed for special duties."—PP 374.

The New Testament church showed the same perfection in its organization. Christ Himself, who formed the church (Matt. 16:18), "set the members, each one of them, in the body just as He pleased" (1 Cor. 12:18). He endowed them with gifts and talents adequate for the functions devolving upon them and organized them into a living, working body, of which He is the head.

"For as we have many members in one body, but all the members do not the same function, so we, being many, are one body in Christ, and individually members of one another" (Rom. 12:4, 5). "And He [Christ] is the head of the body, the church, who is the beginning, the firstborn from the dead, that in all things He may have the preeminence" (Col. 1:18).

"There are diversities of gifts, but the same Spirit. There are differences of ministries, but the same Lord" (1 Cor. 12:4, 5). "For as the body is one and has many members, but all the members of that one body, being many, are one body, so also is Christ" (1 Cor. 12:12). "Now you are the body of Christ, and members individually. And God has appointed these in the church: first apostles, second prophets, third teachers, after that miracles, then gifts of healings, helps, administrations, varieties of tongues" (1 Cor. 12:27, 28).

Importance of Organization

Just as there can be no living, active human body unless its members are organically united and functioning together, so there can be no living, growing, prospering church unless its members are organized into a united spiritual body, all performing their God-given duties and functions under the direction of a divinely constituted authority. Without organization no institution or movement can prosper. A nation without organized government would be chaos. A business enterprise without organization would fail. A church without organization would disintegrate and perish.

For the sake of the Church's healthy development and for the accomplishment of its task of carrying the gospel of salvation to all the world, Christ gave it a simple but effective system of organization. Success in its endeavors to achieve its mission depends on loyal adherence to this divine pattern.

"Some have advanced the thought that as we near the close of time, every child of God will act independently of any religious organization. But I have been instructed by the Lord that in this work there is no such thing as every man's being independent."—TM 489.

"Oh, how Satan would rejoice if he could succeed in his efforts to get in among this people and disorganize the work at a time when thorough organization is essential and will be the greatest power to keep out spurious uprisings and to refute claims not endorsed by the Word of God! We want to hold the lines evenly, that there shall be no breaking down of the system of organization and order that has been built up by wise, careful labor. License must not be given to disorderly elements that desire to control the work at this time."—TM 489.

Purposes of Organization

"As our numbers increased, it was evident that without some form of organization there would be great confusion, and the work would not be carried forward successfully. To provide for the support of the ministry, for carrying the work in new fields, for protecting both the churches and the ministry from unworthy members, for holding church property, for the publication of the truth through the press, and for many other objects, organization was indispensable."—TM 26.

"As members of the visible church, and workers in the vineyard of the Lord, all professed Christians should do their utmost to preserve peace, harmony, and love in the church. Mark the prayer of Christ: 'That they all may be one; as thou, Father, art in me, and I in thee, that they also may be one in us: that the world may believe that thou hast sent me.' The unity of the church is the convincing evidence that God has sent Jesus into the world as its Redeemer."—5T 619, 620.

The New Testament Model

The Savior's commission to the church to carry the gospel to all the world (Matt. 28:19, 20; Mark 16:15) meant not only preaching the gospel but ensuring the welfare of those who accepted that message. This involved shepherding as well as housing the flock, and also meeting relationship problems. Such a situation called for organization.

At first the apostles constituted a council that directed the activities of the church from Jerusalem (Acts 6:2; 8:14). When the company there became so large that the administration of its practical affairs became a problem, the church appointed deacons to care for its business (Acts 6:2-4).

Later other congregations grew up, not only in Asia but also in Europe, and this called for further organizational steps. In Asia Minor elders were ordained "in every church" (Acts 14:23). Extension of the work throughout the various provinces of the Roman Empire called for organization of churches into what might be called conferences (Gal. 1:2). Thus, step by step, organization grew in the early church. As needs arose, God directed the leaders of His work so that, in counsel with the church, they developed a form of organization that safeguarded the interests of the work.

Church Organization Today

The Seventh-day Adventist form of governance is representative, which recognizes that authority rests in the membership and is expressed through duly elected representatives at each level of organization, with executive responsibility delegated to representative bodies and officers for the governing of the Church at each separate level. The *Church Manual* applies this principle of representation to the operations of the local congregation.

Issues of representation in organizations with mission status are defined by operating policies and in organizations with conference status by their constitution and bylaws. This form of governance recognizes also that ordination to the ministry is recognized by the Church worldwide.

"Every member of the church has a voice in choosing officers of the church. The church chooses the officers of the state conferences. Delegates chosen by the state conferences choose the officers of the union conferences, and delegates chosen by the union conferences choose the officers of the General Conference. By this arrangement every conference, every institution, every church, and every individual, either directly or through representatives, has a voice in the election of the men who bear the chief responsibilities in the General Conference."—8T 236, 237.

The present organizational system of the Church resulted from a developing theological understanding of the mission of the Church, membership growth, and the Church's geographic spread. Representatives of conferences met in 1863 to organize the General Conference of Seventh-day Adventists.

There are several organizational levels within the Church leading from the individual believer to the worldwide organization of the work. Membership units in each of these levels periodically convene formal business sessions known as constituency meetings or sessions. (The constituency meeting or session of a local church is generally referred to as a business meeting.) In Seventh-day Adventist Church structure, no organization determines its own status, nor does it function as if it had no obligations to the Church family beyond its boundaries.

Outline of Denominational Organization

1.   Local Church—A group of members in a defined location that has been granted, by the constituency of a conference in session, official status as a church.

2.   Local Conference—A group of local churches, within a defined geographical area, that has been granted, by action of a division executive committee at midyear, year-end, or division council meeting, official status as a Seventh-day Adventist local conference/mission/field and subsequently accepted, at a union constituency meeting, into the sisterhood of conferences/missions. (See p.18.)

3.   Union of Churches—A group of churches, within a defined geographical area, that has been granted, by a General Conference Session,

official status as a union of churches with either conference or mission status.

4.   Union Conference/Mission—A group of conferences, within a defined geographical area, that has been granted, by a General Conference Session, official status as a union conference/mission.

5.   General Conference and Its Divisions—The General Conference represents the worldwide expression of the Church. Its constituent membership is defined in its Constitution. To facilitate its worldwide activity, the General Conference has established regional offices, known as divisions of the General Conference, which have been assigned, by action of the General Conference Executive Committee at Annual Councils, general administrative oversight for designated groups of unions and other Church units within specific geographical areas.

The Bible is the foundation and source of belief and practice; on this basis, the General Conference in Session determines the stated fundamental beliefs of the Church. The General Conference in Session also authorizes establishment of unions and the attachment of field units, revises the *Church Manual*, elects General Conference and division leadership, performs other functions as outlined in its Constitution and Bylaws, and considers items referred to it by its Executive Committee. The General Conference Executive Committee between Sessions is empowered by the Constitution and Bylaws to act on behalf of the constituents. Thus Church organizations around the world recognize the General Conference in Session as the voice of the Church.

Role of Institutions

The constituent levels of the Church operate a variety of educational, health-care, publishing, and other institutions reaching out in the name of Christ to meet the needs of a distraught world. In Seventh-day Adventist theology and philosophy these institutions from their inception have been indispensable instruments for carrying out the Church's spiritual mission of serving the whole person and taking the gospel to the world.

No Church organization or institution assumes responsibility for the liabilities, debts, acts, or omissions of any other Church organization simply because of its Church affiliation.

Authority in the Early Church

As Creator, Redeemer and Sustainer, Lord and King of all creation, God alone is the source of authority for the Church. He delegated authority to His prophets and apostles (2 Cor. 10:8). They, therefore, occupied a crucial and unique position in the transmission of the Word of God and the edification of the church (Eph. 2:20).

The early church bore responsibility for purity in doctrine and practice. The elders (or bishops) held great authority. One of their main functions was general pastoral care and oversight (Acts 20:17-28; Heb. 13:17; 1 Peter 5:1-3), with special tasks such as giving instruction in sound doctrine and refuting those who contradicted it (1 Tim. 3:1, 2; Titus 1:5, 9). They were instructed to "test the spirits, whether they are of God" (1 John 4:1) or, in Paul's terms, to "test all things" and "hold fast what is good" (1 Thess. 5:21).

The same was true regarding its exercise of discipline (Matt. 18:15-17), which ranged from private and caring admonition (cf. Matt. 18:16; Gal. 6:1) to removal from membership (Matt. 18:18; 1 Cor. 5:11, 13; 2 Cor. 2:5-11).

The Church thus has authority to settle the rules for its own governance.

General Conference the Highest Authority

In the Church today the General Conference Session, and the General Conference Executive Committee between Sessions, is the highest ecclesiastical authority in the administration of the Church. The General Conference Executive Committee is authorized by its Constitution to create subordinate organizations with authority to carry out their roles. Therefore all subordinate organizations and institutions throughout the Church will recognize the General Conference Session, and the General Conference Executive Committee between Sessions, as the highest ecclesiastical authority, under God, among Seventh-day Adventists.

When differences arise in or between churches and conferences or institutions, matters that are not mutually resolved may be appealed to the next higher organization. If the matter does not get resolved at this level, the aggrieved entity may appeal to successively higher levels of organization. An organization to which an appeal is forwarded may choose not to hear the matter, in which case the decision of the highest organization involved in the dispute shall be final. When organizations review decisions of other organizations, they do not assume responsibility for the liabilities of any other organization.

"I have often been instructed by the Lord that no man's judgment should be surrendered to the judgment of any other one man. Never should the mind of one man or the minds of a few men be regarded as sufficient in wisdom and power to control the work and to say what plans shall be followed. But when, in a General Conference, the judgment of the brethren assembled from all parts of the field is exercised, private independence and private judgment must not be stubbornly maintained, but surrendered. Never should a laborer regard as a virtue the persistent maintenance of his position of independence, contrary to the decision of the general body."— 9T 260.

CHAPTER 4

Pastors and Other Church Employees

A Divinely Appointed Ministry

"God has a church, and she has a divinely appointed ministry. 'And He gave some, apostles; and some, prophets; and some, evangelists; and some, pastors and teachers; for the perfecting of the saints, for the work of the ministry, for the edifying of the body of Christ: till we all come in the unity of the faith, and of the knowledge of the Son of God, unto a perfect man, unto the measure of the stature of the fullness of Christ. . . . '

"Men appointed of God have been chosen to watch with jealous care, with vigilant perseverance, that the church may not be overthrown by the evil devices of Satan, but that she shall stand in the world to promote the glory of God among men."—TM 52, 53.

Conference President—The conference president should be an ordained pastor of experience and good report. He stands at the head of the gospel ministry in the conference and is the chief elder, or overseer, of all the churches. He works for their spiritual welfare and counsels them regarding their activities and plans. He has access to all the churches and their services, business meetings, and boards, without vote unless granted by the church, or unless he is a member of that congregation. He may, by virtue of his office, preside over any meeting of any church when necessary. He has access to all church records.

The conference president does not have authority to set aside the duly elected officers of the church, but will work in cooperation with them. They in turn are bound, in recognition of the ties of conference fellowship, to counsel with him over all that pertains to the welfare of the church. They should not attempt to exclude him from a proper discharge of his duties.

Conference Departmental Directors—Conference departmental directors foster important lines of denominational work under the general direction of the conference committee in consultation with the conference president. In order to successfully carry on the work assigned to them, these employees must have access to the churches so they can present and develop their plans. These employees will have sympathetic consideration for all church plans, even outside their respective departments.

Departmental directors are not vested with administrative or executive authority, so their relation to local churches is advisory. Their work does not bear the same relationship to the churches as that of the conference committee or president. In the promotion of their specific kinds of work, they labor throughout the entire conference. However, they are not expected to counsel churches regarding elections and other administrative duties or any other line of service, unless especially requested to do so by the conference president.

Ordained Pastors—Ordained pastors appointed by the conference committee to act as pastors or district leaders do not take the place of the president in their respective fields. They are not charged with administrative powers as is the president, but they cooperate with him in carrying out the plans and policies of the conference.

On assignment to a local church, the ordained pastor is assisted by the local elders. By virtue of ordination, the pastor is qualified to function in all rites and ceremonies. The pastor should be the congregation's spiritual leader and adviser. Pastors should instruct the officers in their duties and plan with them for all lines of church work and activity.

The pastor is a member of the church board and serves as its chairperson. If the pastor desires to be relieved of the responsibility of acting as chairperson of the board, an elder serves as chairperson in cooperation with the pastor. (See p. 74.) The pastor, with the assistance of the elders, is expected to plan for and lead out in all spiritual services, such as Sabbath morning worship and prayer meeting, and should officiate at the communion service and baptism. Pastors should not surround themselves with any special body of counselors of their own choosing, but always cooperate with the elected officers.

When an evangelist is asked to conduct an evangelistic effort where there is a church, the conference should invite the pastor to assist the evangelist, thus giving the pastor an opportunity to become acquainted with prospective members.

Pastors or assistant pastors are not nominated or elected to such positions by the church. Their connection with the church is by appointment of the conference committee, and such appointments may be changed at any time. (See p. 74.)

A pastor may be removed from office by conference committee action without the individual's church membership being affected. But when a pastor is removed from church membership and subsequently restored to membership as a layperson, the pastor's membership restoration does not mean restoration to the ministry.

Licensed Pastors—To give individuals an opportunity to demonstrate their call to the ministry, especially in the area of soul winning, prospective candidates are granted pastoral licenses by the conference. The granting of such licenses confers the opportunity to develop the ministerial gift.

Licensed pastors are authorized to preach, to engage in evangelism, to lead out in outreach (missionary) work, and to assist in all church activities.

There are circumstances, however, where it is necessary for the conference to appoint a licensed pastor to carry responsibility as a pastor or assistant pastor of a church or group of churches. In order to open the way for a licensed pastor to perform certain pastoral functions, the church or group of churches being served must elect the pastor as a local elder. Then, since the right to permit the extension of a licensed pastor's authority rests first with the division executive committee, it must approve the extension by specifically and clearly defining the additional functions that that licensed pastor may perform. The extended functions are limited only to the church or group of churches where the pastor is assigned and is an elder. After the division committee acts, the conference committee may act. (See p. 74.)

The conference committee shall not extend the functions of a licensed pastor beyond what has been authorized by the division committee. It also shall not authorize a licensed pastor to perform the extended functions in any church beyond where the licensed pastor is assigned and is an elder. A conference committee action cannot be substituted for church election or ordination to gospel ministry.

Bible Instructors—The conference may employ Bible instructors and assign them to work with evangelistic efforts or with local congregations. Though the instructors work under the general direction of the conference, an instructor assigned to an evangelistic effort works under the direction of the evangelist conducting the campaign, and an instructor assigned to a church works under the direction of the pastor. An instructor should not, except by special arrangement with the conference, be asked to carry a church office, but should be left free to carry on soul-winning work.

Conference Directs Church Employees—The conference president in counsel with the conference committee directs all conference employees, such as pastors, Bible instructors, and departmental directors, who receive their credentials from and are responsible to the conference, not the local church. A church may ask the conference president for the services or help of conference employees, but appointments in all cases rest with the conference committee. The conference committee may change employee assignments whenever it believes they are needed. The employee or the church may appeal to the conference committee for a hearing on the decision to remove the employee, and the committee will carefully consider the appeal in light of the needs of the entire conference. If the employee refuses to cooperate with the committee and declines to work in harmony with its decisions, the committee may regard the employee's conduct as insubordination and may deal with it accordingly. In no case should the employee appeal to the church regarding such decisions. If a local church supports an employee's refusal to cooperate, it also becomes subject to conference discipline.

Credentials and Licenses

God's work is to be jealously safeguarded by responsible leaders from the local church to the General Conference. Official credentials and licenses are issued to all authorized full-time Church employees and are granted by controlling committees for limited periods.

In a local conference, the committee confers authority upon individuals to represent the Church as pastors and gospel workers. This authority is represented by the granting of credentials and licenses, which are written commissions, properly dated and signed by the officers of the conference. The authority thus conveyed is not personal or inherent in the individual but is inherent in the granting body, which may recall the credentials for cause at any time. Credentials and licenses granted employees are not their personal property and must be returned when employment is terminated or at the request of the organization that issued them.

No one should be allowed to speak to any congregation unless he/she has been invited by the church in harmony with guidelines given by the conference. It is recognized, however, that there are times when congregations may be addressed by government officials or civic leaders; but all unauthorized persons shall not be given access to the pulpit. (See pp. 118-121.)

Expired Credentials and Licenses—Credentials and licenses are granted for the duration of the term as provided for by the conference constitution and bylaws or operating policy and are renewed by a vote of the conference in session or by the executive committee. Possession of an expired credential or license gives the person no authority whatsoever.

Retired Employees—Retired employees deserve honor and consideration for helping build up God's church. They may continue to bless and help the congregations where they hold membership through election to any office. They also may exercise pastoral functions under the direction of the conference committee.

Former Pastors Without Credentials—Individuals previously ordained as pastors but who no longer have valid credentials may be elected as elders and, if their ordinations have not been invalidated, need not be ordained as elders. Their services are limited to the functions of a local elder.

CHAPTER 5

Organizing, Uniting, and Dissolving Churches and Companies

Organizing a Church

A church is organized by an ordained pastor on the recommendation of the conference executive committee. (For the procedure for organizing a company, see pp. 37, 38.) Since so much is involved in the organization of a church, the local conference president should be invited to be present.

When a company of baptized believers is prepared to assume the responsibilities of an organized church, it must consult with the conference president and obtain approval from the conference executive committee prior to seeking a date for the organization to take place.

When the baptized believers assemble on the agreed-upon date, the individual officiating should first present a brief review of the fundamental beliefs of Seventh-day Adventists.

Then the one presiding should make a call asking all who are in agreement with these principles and who desire to unite in church fellowship to come forward. The name of each person should be recorded. If any are already members of the conference church or another congregation, the one officiating should present the letters of transfers they have secured. Those transferring form the nucleus of the congregation.

If, however, there are no transferring members, then three members (preferably established Sabbathkeepers among those present) should be selected as a nucleus. They may be asked these questions: Do you accept Christ as your personal Savior? Are you in full harmony with the principles of faith that have just been presented? Have you been baptized by immersion? Are you in regular standing and enjoying one another's confidence?

If they answer these questions in the affirmative, the three are declared the nucleus of the new church. Then one after another the names that were recorded are called, each person is asked the questions listed in the preceding paragraph, and the presiding person takes a vote among the nucleus to receive each individual into church fellowship. Each person thus received becomes a member of the church and is qualified to vote on the next name. Care should be taken to see that full fellowship and brotherly love exist among those received into membership. Should any difficulty arise in any case over a question either of doctrine or of fellowship, action should be deferred unless the matter can be adjusted kindly and tactfully.

When the nucleus has voted on all potential members, the church is a complete entity and ready for election of officers. Members then should choose a nominating committee, with the officiating pastor serving as chairperson. The nominating committee brings in nominations to fill the various church offices. When these have been elected, the elders should be ordained, unless they have already been ordained as elders. A similar but shorter service should take place for ordination of deacons and deaconesses. The church then is fully organized and ready for service.

Before the organizing meeting ends, the members should vote to request the conference to receive the newly organized church into the sisterhood of churches at the next conference session.

To maximize success of the new congregation, conference and local leaders should see that all officers are fully instructed concerning their duties. The church also should have the materials needed for the communion service, which, if possible, should be celebrated as part of the organizational meeting. The treasurer, the clerk, and the other officers should receive all the necessary records or equipment needed to carry out their responsibilities.

Organizing a Company

Where a number of isolated believers reside near one another or where they belong to a small group, house church, or church planting core group, they should consider forming a company of believers for fellowship, worship, and mission with the objective of growing into an organized church or multiplying house churches in that geographical area.

Company status is approved by vote of the conference committee, which, should it become necessary, may subsequently dissolve the company. The division and/or conference should have written guidelines for organizing companies within its territory.

Church members who are part of small groups or house groups may form the nucleus of a new company. Membership of all those who want to be part of a company should be held in either the conference church or a local church (mother church). If membership for those who want to be part of a company is to be held in the conference church, the conference committee will vote their membership transfers to the conference church and indicate that they are part of the new company.

When the conference committee approves establishment of a company, a leadership team should be appointed, including a leader, a clerk, and a treasurer. The appointment should be carried out by the district pastor, or other pastor appointed by the conference committee, in counsel with the group being established as a company.

All other company appointments should be made by vote of those who are part of the group that is forming the company. The district pastor or other person authorized by the conference committee shall preside at such a meeting. Only members of the Seventh-day Adventist Church in regular standing shall be appointed.

The leader of a company shall not be ordained to that office and does not have the authority to perform those functions that are vested in an elder of a church. However, where exceptional circumstances warrant, the conference committee may appoint a person of church experience and leadership ability to serve as elder of the company.

The clerk of the company shall keep record of all activities and meetings of the company and shall send regular statistical reports to the mother church or the conference executive secretary. These reports should include statistics on attendance and activities of the company, including outreach ministries conducted during the week or on Sabbath.

The treasurer of the company shall keep record of all money received and disbursed and shall send promptly, at the time established by the conference, all tithes and offerings, other than funds collected for local purposes, to the conference treasurer, who also is treasurer of the conference church.

If the members of an organized company are members of the conference church, the company does not possess the right to administer discipline or transfer or receive members. All such matters must be referred to the conference committee, which constitutes the board of the conference church. The conference president is the elder of the conference church.

If the conference organizes a company through a neighboring mother church instead of through the conference church, the functions listed above (such as reporting and membership) would be cared for by/through the mother church.

Since a company should want to grow and eventually be recognized as a church, its leadership should prepare members for church status by promoting all activities generally carried on by a church.

Uniting Churches

When it is advisable to unite two churches, the conference committee should recommend such a course. In a duly called meeting, presided over by the conference president or the pastor or other ordained pastor, each church should vote on the question of union. When favorable action has been taken by both churches, a joint meeting of the two churches should be arranged, with the conference president presiding or in his absence an ordained pastor appointed by the conference.

A carefully written statement of agreement should be prepared setting forth the reasons for uniting and stating any special matters or conditions involved, such as the disposal of property and responsibility for financial obligations. It should provide for the new name of the united church and for the release from service of all officers of the two churches.

Adoption of the agreement by the united body consummates the union of the two churches. Members of the new congregation then should choose a nominating committee to nominate officers to serve for the remainder of the current year.

A copy of the agreement should then be filed with the conference.

The entire membership of both churches unites in the new organization. It is not permissible to remove any members by failing to include them in the membership list at the time of uniting. The united body becomes responsible for the order and discipline of all members. Members under discipline should be dealt with as provided elsewhere in this manual.

All records of both churches become a part of the records of the united body. The local conference should be notified so that it may take suitable actions at its next session.

Dissolving or Expelling Churches

"Christ also loved the church and gave Himself for her, that He might sanctify and cleanse her with the washing of water by the word, that He might present her to Himself a glorious church, not having spot or wrinkle or any such thing, but that she should be holy and without blemish. . . . For no one ever hated his own flesh, but nourishes and cherishes it, just as the Lord does the church. For we are members of His body, of His flesh and of His bones" (Eph. 5:25-30).

This spirit should permeate all efforts to help an erring church and all aspects of any discipline that may be applied—always to help and save for the cause of God.

Church status is not necessarily perpetual. A church may be dissolved or expelled from the sisterhood of churches for the following reasons:

1.   **Loss of Members**—Occasionally, despite efforts to preserve a church, so many members are lost by moving away or by death or by apostasy that the existence of the church is threatened. Under such circumstances the conference committee should recommend possible dissolution of the church.

Before a church takes final action to dissolve, the remaining members shall be invited to transfer their memberships to other churches.

If enough members remain, the congregation may call a business meeting, presided over by the conference president or by a pastor designated by him, to vote to approve letters requesting transfer of all members in regular standing to unite with other churches. In this way the church dissolves itself upon recommendation of the conference committee, and the way is opened for the conference committee to take action recording dissolution of the church.

If, in the judgment of the conference committee, there are too few members available to call a business meeting, the conference committee shall have the authority to recommend transfer of members in regular standing to other churches or to the conference church. In this way the church is dissolved.

If at the time of dissolution there are members who are under discipline and therefore cannot be granted letters saying they are in regular standing, their memberships shall be provisionally held in the conference church while conference administration ensures that every effort is made as soon as possible to help such members to a satisfactory Christian experience. If the efforts are successful, their memberships may then be confirmed in the conference church or letters granted to them for transfer to other churches. If they cannot be reclaimed, they should be removed from membership by vote of the conference committee.

2.   **Discipline**—Occasions for expelling churches for disciplinary reasons are rare because the mission of the church is to seek and to save. Where serious problems such as apostasy, refusal to operate in harmony with the *Church Manual*, or rebellion against the conference persist, earnest efforts should be made to avert the need for expulsion. The pastor should seek to deepen the spiritual life of the church through preaching and personal visitation ministries. The conference should encourage a series of revival meetings to lead the members to renew their covenant with their Lord. If these efforts are unsuccessful, the pastor, in cooperation with the

conference committee, should counsel with the church and its leadership, seeking to bring healing and reconciliation and to preserve the church.

Such remedial measures are preferable to permitting the deterioration of relationships, which could lead to expulsion of the church.

However, if all efforts to preserve the church fail, the conference committee should give careful study to the question of expulsion. If such action is decided upon, the conference shall follow the following procedure:

    a.   The decision to recommend expulsion, with supporting reasons, shall be presented to the church itself in a business meeting for its information and consideration.

    b.   If the church does not accept the recommendation, it may respond in one of the following ways:

    1)   Eliminating the causes for discipline and accepting the conference specifications, request the conference to rescind the recommendation to dissolve or expel.

    2)   Appeal to the union executive committee, or to the division in case of a union of churches, to arbitrate on behalf of the church.

    c.   If the church remains in rebellion, the conference executive committee makes a recommendation to a regular or specially called constituency meeting that the church be dissolved.

    d.   If the constituency takes action to expel, the conference shall enforce the decision.

Care of Members, Records, and Funds

Loyal members of a dissolved or expelled church may desire to retain their memberships in the Church. To ensure their welfare, their memberships shall be provisionally held for up to one year in the conference church to allow opportunity for those who desire to have their memberships in the conference church confirmed or transferred to another church. Their standing shall be evaluated by the conference committee, and, if satisfactory, the conference committee may recommend them for membership in the conference church or churches of their choice.

The names of members of a dissolved or expelled church who are under discipline shall be referred to the conference secretary for early attention by the conference committee as set out in "Loss of Members," above.

On dissolution or expulsion of a church for loss of members or for disciplinary reasons, all offerings, financial accounts, and all property real or personal, whether held in the name of the local church or the conference or other denominational legal association, are held in trust for the conference. The conference therefore has the right, the authority, and the duty to administer, protect, or dispose of such property and funds. All records of the church are to be held in the custody of the conference secretary and/or treasurer.

In cases where discipline is not involved, an alternative to dissolving or expelling a church is to return it to company status. Such a decision will be made by a majority vote of the conference committee, following consultation with the district pastor and members, and conveyed to the church by the pastor or conference representative.

At a business meeting (see pp. 40, 41), letters of transfer may be voted to all remaining members in regular standing to the conference church or to other churches in the cases of any members who wish to transfer. At the same meeting, the pastor, in counsel with the local members, shall appoint from the members of the new company a leadership team, including a leader, a clerk, and a treasurer. For details of other organizational matters relating to a company, see "Organizing a Company" on pp. 37, 38.

CHAPTER 6

Membership

The solemn obligations of membership in the body of Christ should be impressed on everyone desiring Church membership. Only those giving evidence of having experienced the new birth and enjoying a spiritual experience in the Lord Jesus are prepared for acceptance into membership. Pastors must instruct candidates in the fundamental teachings and related practices of the Church so they will enter the Church on a sound spiritual basis. While there is no stated age for baptism, it is recommended that very young children who express a desire to be baptized should be encouraged and entered into an instruction program that may lead to baptism.

The apostle Paul writes: "Or do you not know that as many of us as were baptized into Christ Jesus were baptized into His death? Therefore we were buried with Him through baptism into death, that just as Christ was raised from the dead by the glory of the Father, even so we also should walk in newness of life" (Rom. 6:3, 4).

Luke also reports: "Then Peter said to them, 'Repent, and let every one of you be baptized in the name of Jesus Christ.' . . . Then those who gladly received his word were baptized; and that day about three thousand souls were added to them" (Acts 2:38-41).

"The members of the church, those whom He has called out of darkness into His marvelous light, are to show forth His glory. The church is the repository of the riches of the grace of Christ; and through the church will eventually be made manifest, even to 'the principalities and powers in heavenly places,' the final and full display of the love of God."—AA 9.

Baptism

A Prerequisite to Membership—"Christ has made baptism the sign of entrance to His spiritual kingdom. He has made this a positive condition with which all must comply who wish to be acknowledged as under the authority of the Father, the Son, and the Holy Spirit. . . .

"Baptism is a most solemn renunciation of the world. Those who are baptized in the threefold name of the Father, the Son, and the Holy Spirit, at the very entrance of their Christian life declare publicly that they have forsaken the service of Satan and have become members of the royal family, children of the heavenly King. They have obeyed the command: 'Come out from among them, and be ye separate, . . . and touch not the unclean thing.' And to them is fulfilled the promise: 'I will receive you, and will be a Father unto you, and ye shall be My sons and daughters, saith the Lord Almighty.' 2 Corinthians 6:17, 18."—6T 91.

Baptism is the avenue of induction into the Church. It is fundamentally the pledge of entrance into Christ's saving covenant and should be treated as a solemn and yet joyful welcome into the family of God.

Membership in the Church is possible only in those churches included in the sisterhood of churches recognized by a conference.

Mode of Baptism—The Church believes in baptism by immersion and accepts into membership only those who have been baptized in this manner. (See Chapter 14, "Fundamental Beliefs of Seventh-day Adventists.") Those who acknowledge their lost state as sinners, sincerely repent of their sins, and experience conversion may, after proper instruction, be accepted as candidates for baptism and Church membership.

Thorough Instruction and Public Examination Before Baptism— Candidates individually or in a baptismal class should be instructed from the Scriptures regarding the Church's fundamental beliefs and practices and the responsibilities of membership. A pastor should satisfy the church by a public examination that candidates are well instructed, are committed to taking this important step, and by practice and conduct demonstrate a willing acceptance of Church doctrines and the principles of conduct which are the outward expression of those doctrines, for "by their fruits you will know them" (Matt. 7:20).

If public examination is impractical, then candidates should be examined by the board or a committee appointed by the board, such as the board of elders, whose report then should be given to the church before the baptism.

"The test of discipleship is not brought to bear as closely as it should be upon those who present themselves for baptism. It should be understood whether they are simply taking the name of Seventh-day Adventists, or whether they are taking their stand on the Lord's side, to come out from the world and be separate, and touch not the unclean thing. Before baptism there should be a thorough inquiry as to the experience of the candidates. Let this inquiry be made, not in a cold and distant way, but kindly, tenderly, pointing the new converts to the Lamb of God that taketh away the sin of the world. Bring the requirements of the gospel to bear upon the candidates for baptism."—6T 95, 96.

Baptismal Vow and Commitment

Baptismal Vow—Baptismal candidates and those being received into fellowship by profession of faith shall affirm their acceptance of the fundamental beliefs in the presence of the local congregation or other properly appointed body. (See p. 44.)

The pastor or elder should address the following questions to the candidate(s), whose reply may be by verbal assent, raising the hand, or other culturally appropriate method.

Vow

1. Do you believe there is one God: Father, Son, and Holy Spirit, a unity of three coeternal Persons?

2. Do you accept the death of Jesus Christ on Calvary as the atoning sacrifice for your sins and believe that by God's grace through faith in His shed blood you are saved from sin and its penalty?

3. Do you accept Jesus Christ as your Lord and personal Savior, believing that God, in Christ, has forgiven your sins and given you a new heart, and do you renounce the sinful ways of the world?

4. Do you accept by faith the righteousness of Christ, your Intercessor in the heavenly sanctuary, and accept His promise of transforming grace and power to live a loving, Christ-centered life in your home and before the world?

5. Do you believe that the Bible is God's inspired Word, the only rule of faith and practice for the Christian? Do you covenant to spend time regularly in prayer and Bible study?

6. Do you accept the Ten Commandments as a transcript of the character of God and a revelation of His will? Is it your purpose by the power of the indwelling Christ to keep this law, including the fourth commandment, which requires the observance of the seventh day of the week as the Sabbath of the Lord and the memorial of Creation?

7. Do you look forward to the soon coming of Jesus and the blessed hope, when "this mortal shall . . . put on immortality" [1 Cor. 15:54, KJV]? As you prepare to meet the Lord, will you witness to His loving salvation by using your talents in personal soul-winning endeavor to help others to be ready for His glorious appearing?

8.   Do you accept the biblical teaching of spiritual gifts and believe that the gift of prophecy is one of the identifying marks of the remnant church?

9.   Do you believe in Church organization? Is it your purpose to worship God and to support the Church through your tithes and offerings and by your personal effort and influence?

10. Do you believe that your body is the temple of the Holy Spirit; and will you honor God by caring for it, avoiding the use of that which is harmful, and abstaining from all unclean foods; from the use, manufacture, or sale of alcoholic beverages; from the use, manufacture, or sale of tobacco in any of its forms for human consumption; and from the misuse of or trafficking in narcotics or other drugs?

11. Do you know and understand the fundamental Bible principles as taught by the Seventh-day Adventist Church? Do you purpose, by the grace of God, to fulfill His will by ordering your life in harmony with these principles?

12. Do you accept the New Testament teaching of baptism by immersion and desire to be so baptized as a public expression of faith in Christ and His forgiveness of your sins?

13. Do you accept and believe that the Seventh-day Adventist Church is the remnant church of Bible prophecy and that people of every nation, race, and language are invited and accepted into its fellowship? Do you desire to be a member of this local congregation of the world Church?

Alternative Vow

1.   Do you accept Jesus Christ as your personal Savior and Lord, and do you desire to live your life in a saving relationship with Him?

2.   Do you accept the teachings of the Bible as expressed in the Statement of Fundamental Beliefs of the Seventh-day Adventist Church, and do you pledge by God's grace to live your life in harmony with these teachings?

3.   Do you desire to be baptized as a public expression of your belief in Jesus Christ, to be accepted into the fellowship of the Seventh-day Adventist Church, and to support the Church and its mission as a faithful steward by your personal influence, tithes and offerings, and a life of service?

Baptismal Covenant—The Church has adopted its 28 fundamental beliefs, together with the baptismal vow and Certificate of Baptism and Commitment, as a baptismal covenant.

A printed copy of this covenant, with the Certificate of Baptism and Commitment properly completed, should be given to all accepted into membership by baptism. An appropriate certificate also should be given those accepted on profession of faith.

The Certificate of Baptism and Commitment contains a space for the new member to sign as an affirmation of commitment. Following the baptism, the Certificate of Baptism and Commitment should be presented to the candidate as a covenant document. The commitment reads as follows:

Commitment

1. I believe there is one God: Father, Son, and Holy Spirit, a unity of three coeternal Persons.

2. I accept the death of Jesus Christ on Calvary as the atoning sacrifice for my sins and believe that by God's grace through faith in His shed blood I am saved from sin and its penalty.

3. I accept Jesus Christ as my Lord and personal Savior and believe that God, in Christ, has forgiven my sins and given me a new heart, and I renounce the sinful ways of the world.

4. I accept by faith the righteousness of Christ, my Intercessor in the heavenly sanctuary, and accept His promise of transforming grace and power to live a loving, Christ-centered life in my home and before the world.

5. I believe that the Bible is God's inspired Word, the only rule of faith and practice for the Christian. I covenant to spend time regularly in prayer and Bible study.

6. I accept the Ten Commandments as a transcript of the character of God and a revelation of His will. It is my purpose by the power of the indwelling Christ to keep this law, including the fourth commandment, which requires the observance of the seventh day of the week as the Sabbath of the Lord and the memorial of Creation.

7. I look forward to the soon coming of Jesus and the blessed hope, when "this mortal shall . . . put on immortality" [1 Cor. 15:54, KJV]. As I prepare to meet the Lord, I will witness to His loving salvation by using my talents in personal soul-winning endeavor to help others to be ready for His glorious appearing.

8.   I accept the biblical teaching of spiritual gifts and believe that the gift of prophecy is one of the identifying marks of the remnant church.

9.   I believe in Church organization. It is my purpose to worship God and to support the Church through my tithes and offerings and by my personal effort and influence.

10.   I believe that my body is the temple of the Holy Spirit; and I will honor God by caring for it, avoiding the use of that which is harmful, and abstaining from all unclean foods; from the use, manufacture, or sale of alcoholic beverages; from the use, manufacture, or sale of tobacco in any of its forms for human consumption; and from the misuse of or trafficking in narcotics or other drugs.

11.   I know and understand the fundamental Bible principles as taught by the Seventh-day Adventist Church. I purpose, by the grace of God, to fulfill His will by ordering my life in harmony with these principles.

12.   I accept the New Testament teaching of baptism by immersion and desire to be so baptized as a public expression of faith in Christ and His forgiveness of my sins.

13.   I accept and believe that the Seventh-day Adventist Church is the remnant church of Bible prophecy and that people of every nation, race, and language are invited and accepted into its fellowship. I desire to be a member of this local congregation of the world Church.

Voting Acceptance Subject to Baptism—After the candidates have, in the presence of the church membership or other properly appointed body, answered the questions of the vow in the affirmative, or assurance has been given to the church that they have already done so, the church should vote on their acceptance into membership subject to baptism, which should not be unduly delayed.

Receiving Members Who Are Not Known—In preparing for the baptism of converts, an evangelist should invite the pastor or elder to visit the baptismal class to become acquainted with the candidates. Such contacts will enable the church to be better prepared to receive the new members.

Baptismal Preparations—At the baptismal ceremony the deacons should make necessary preparations and also assist male candidates into and out of the water. The deaconesses should assist female candidates.

Care should be exercised to see that proper attire is provided for the candidates, preferably robes of suitable heavy material. If robes are not available, the candidates should dress in modest attire.

The baptism should be followed by a short welcoming ceremony.

Rebaptism

Rebaptism is specifically mentioned only in Acts 19:1-7, where the apostle Paul endorsed it for a group of believers whose previous baptism of repentance had been by John. In addition to repentance, Christian baptism is associated with an understanding of and personal commitment to the gospel and the teachings of Jesus and a reception of the Holy Spirit. With this increased understanding and commitment, rebaptism is acceptable.

Individuals From Other Christian Communions—On biblical grounds, individuals from other Christian communions who have embraced Seventh- day Adventist beliefs and who have previously been baptized by immersion may request rebaptism.

The following examples, however, suggest that rebaptism may not be required. Evidently the instance of Acts 19 was a special one, for Apollos is reported to have received John's baptism (Acts 18:25), and there is no record that he was rebaptized. Apparently some of the apostles themselves received John's baptism (John 1:35-40), but there is no record they were rebaptized.

If a new believer has accepted significant new truths, Ellen G. White supports rebaptism as the Spirit leads the new believer to request it. This follows the developmental pattern of Acts 19. An individual who has previously experienced baptism by immersion should evaluate his/her new religious experience and determine whether he/she desires rebaptism. There is to be no urging.

"This [rebaptism] is a subject which each individual must conscientiously take his position upon in the fear of God. This subject should be carefully presented in the spirit of tenderness and love. Then the duty of urging belongs to no one but God; give God a chance to work with His Holy Spirit upon the minds, so that the individual will be perfectly convinced and satisfied in regard to this advanced step."—Ev 373.

Apostasy and Rebaptism—Although apostasy existed in the apostolic church (Heb. 6:4-6), Scripture does not address the question of rebaptism. Ellen G. White supports rebaptism when members have apostatized and then are reconverted and wish to rejoin the Church. (See pp. 66, 67, 154.)

"The Lord calls for a decided reformation. And when a soul is truly reconverted, let him be rebaptized. Let him renew his covenant with God, and God will renew His covenant with him."—Ev 375.

Inappropriate Rebaptism—On the basis of biblical teaching and the guidance of Ellen G. White, rebaptism should occur only in special circumstances and should be relatively rare. To administer baptism repeatedly or on an emotional basis lessens its meaning and represents a misunderstanding of the gravity and significance that Scripture assigns to it. A member whose spiritual experience has become cold needs a spirit of repentance which leads to revival and reformation. This experience will be followed by participation in the communion service to signify renewed cleansing and fellowship in the body of Christ, making rebaptism unnecessary.

Profession of Faith

Individuals who have accepted the fundamental beliefs of the Seventh-day Adventist Church and who desire membership in the Church on profession of faith may be accepted under any of the following four circumstances:

1.   A committed Christian coming from another Christian communion who has already been baptized by immersion as practiced by the Seventh-day Adventist Church. (See p. 44.)

2.   A member of the Seventh-day Adventist Church who, because of world conditions, is unable to secure a letter of transfer from his/her home church. (See p. 53.)

3.   A member of the Seventh-day Adventist Church whose request for membership transfer has received no response from the church where he/she is a member. In such a case the church shall seek assistance of the conference or conferences involved.

4.   An individual who has been a member, but whose membership has been misplaced or has been withdrawn because he/she was a missing member, yet who has remained faithful to his/her Christian commitment.

Great care should be exercised in receiving members if they have formerly been members of another congregation. When a person applies for membership on profession of faith, inquiries should be made concerning the applicant's former experience. Church officers should seek the advice and help of the conference president. Sufficient time should be taken to investigate the facts.

When a person applies for membership on profession of faith and it is found that he/she still is a member of another congregation, no steps should be taken to receive that person into membership until the church holding the membership grants a letter of transfer. If, after the process of transfer is followed (see pp. 51, 52), a church refuses to grant a letter of transfer and the member feels the letter has been unjustly denied, the member may appeal to the conference committee. Following this procedure will result in a higher appreciation of the sacredness of Church membership and in wrongs being made right. No church has the right to withhold transfer unless the person is under discipline.

When an individual whose membership has been removed seeks readmission to church membership, readmission is normally preceded by rebaptism. (See pp. 67, 68.)

Transferring Members

When members move to a different area, the clerk of the church holding their membership records should write to the secretary of the relevant conference requesting that a pastor in the new locality visit them and help facilitate their membership transfer to the new congregation.

The clerk of the church holding the membership records also should notify the transferring members of the intention to give their new addresses to the conference.

Members who move to another locality for longer than six months should make immediate applications for letters of transfer. Members moving to an isolated area with no church within a reasonable distance should apply to join the conference church.

Method of Granting Letters of Transfer—Members should apply for their letters of transfer to the clerk of the church with which the members desire to unite (the receiving church). That clerk sends the request to the clerk of the church from which the members desire to transfer (the granting church). (For alternative method, see p. 52.)

When the clerk of the granting church receives the request, the clerk brings it to the pastor or elder, who in turn presents it to the board. After due consideration, the board votes to recommend, favorably or otherwise, to the church. (See pp. 36-38, 40, 49-55, 65-68, 82.) The pastor or elder then brings the recommendation to the attention of the church for a first reading. Final action is taken the following week, when the request is presented to the church for a vote.

The purpose of the one-week interval is to give members an opportunity to object to the granting of the letter. Objections ordinarily should not be publicly stated but be lodged with the pastor or elder, who then refers them to the board for consideration. The board should give each objector opportunity to appear to present his/her objection. If the objection is not based on valid grounds, the person raising objection should be admonished to withdraw it. If the objection is based on valid grounds, it is the duty of the board to investigate. Final action on granting the letter is deferred until the matter has been satisfactorily settled.

If the objection involves personal relationships, every effort should be made to effect reconciliation. If public offenses are involved, disciplinary measures may be called for. If there is some spiritual lapse, efforts should be made to restore the member.

Clerk to Prepare Letter—When the church has granted the letter of transfer, the clerk fills out the regular transfer form and forwards it to the clerk of the receiving church. The clerk of the receiving church then passes the letter to the pastor or elder, who presents it first to the board for recommendation, after which the request is presented to the church at its next regular service. The vote accepting the person into membership usually is taken at the regular service one week later. The clerk of the receiving church then adds the member's name and date of admittance to the membership record. The clerk also fills out the return portion of the letter of transfer, certifying that the member has been accepted, and returns it to the clerk of the granting church. (See p. 82.)

Letter Valid Six Months—A letter of transfer is valid for six months from date of issue.

Alternative Method for Membership Transfer—A division may approve alternative methods for transferring members between churches within the division, but when members request transfers to a church in another division, the above "Method of Granting Letters of Transfer" must be followed.

Membership During Transfer—Under no circumstances shall the clerk of the granting church remove a member's name from the membership record until the return portion of the transfer letter has been received, certifying that the member has been voted into the fellowship of the receiving church. To do so deprives the person of membership during the transfer. The clerk, the elders, the pastor, and the conference president are all responsible for seeing that all churches adhere to this procedure.

Receiving Members Under Difficult Conditions—World conditions sometimes prevent communications concerning a membership transfer. In such situations, the receiving church, in counsel with the conference, should satisfy itself as to the applicant's standing and then receive him/her into membership on profession of faith. If the way later opens to communicate with the granting church or to the conference where it is located, the receiving church should send a letter stating what it has done.

Counted in Statistical Reports—When quarterly and annual statistical reports are made, a member to whom a letter has been granted, but whose return certificate has not been received, is counted as a member of the granting church. When the return certificate has been received, the name is then removed from the membership record of the granting church and not included in subsequent reports.

If Member Is Not Accepted—The receiving church must receive the member unless it knows a valid reason it should not extend the privilege of membership. If a church does not receive the member, the clerk should return the letter to the granting church with a full explanation of the reasons. The person's membership then remains with the granting church, which should cooperate with the member to resolve the matter.

Letters Granted Only to Those in Regular Standing—Letters of transfer are granted only to members in regular standing, never to a member under discipline. Qualifying statements are out of order except when the pastor or board of the granting church has factual or proven knowledge that the member has been involved as a perpetrator of child abuse. In that case, for the safety of children, the pastor or elder should provide a confidential statement alerting the pastor or elder of the congregation to which the member is transferring.

If a member who has moved to a new location has grown indifferent, the pastor or elder of the granting church may, to be clear in the matter before the transfer is granted, take up the question with the pastor or elder of the receiving church.

No Letter Without Member's Approval—In no case should a church vote a letter of transfer contrary to the desire of the member, nor should a church accept a member by a letter granted under such circumstances. Membership is the personal relationship of an individual to the body of Christ, and a church should recognize this relationship and avoid any action that might be construed as arbitrary.

On the other hand, a member is under obligation to recognize the welfare of the church and to make every effort to relieve the church of problems incident to absentee members. When a member moves, he/she should promptly request a letter of transfer.

When a church is expelled from the sisterhood of churches by action of a conference session, the memberships of all loyal members, except those who refuse, are considered moved to the conference church on a provisional basis. The conference church then may issue letters of transfer for loyal members and deal with other memberships as may be necessary. (See pp. 39-42.)

Church Board Cannot Grant Letters—A board has no authority to vote letters of transfer or to receive members by letter. The board's authority is limited to making recommendations to the church. Action on all transfers of membership, favorable or otherwise, must be taken by the church. (See pp. 51, 52.) The clerk has no authority to remove names from or add names to the membership record except by vote of the church, unless a member requests in writing to be removed from church membership, in which case the church board must act on the request. Efforts should be made to restore the individual to the church family. When a member dies, the clerk records the date of death in the membership record, and no action by the church is necessary.

Membership in the Conference Church—Isolated members should unite with the conference church, which is a body organized for the benefit of believers who otherwise would be without church privileges. Aged and infirmed members who live near a church and conference officers and other employees, including pastors, should be members of a local church, not the conference church.

The conference president is the presiding elder of the conference church, and the work normally carried by the clerk and the treasurer is handled by the conference secretary and treasurer. Since the church has no board, all business normally conducted by a local church board is conducted by the conference committee, which also appoints delegates from the conference church to the conference session.

Membership Record—The church should have one membership record. Names are added or removed only on the vote of the church or at death. (See pp. 81, 82.) Under no circumstances should a church keep a retired membership list.

CHAPTER 7

Discipline

General Principles

The Bible and the Spirit of Prophecy set forth in clear, unmistakable language the solemn responsibility that rests upon the people of God to maintain their purity, integrity, and spiritual fervor. If members grow indifferent or drift away, the church must seek to reclaim them for the Lord.

Dealing With Erring Members—"Moreover if your brother sins against you, go and tell him his fault between you and him alone. If he hears you, you have gained your brother. But if he will not hear, take with you one or two more, that 'by the mouth of two or three witnesses every word may be established.' And if he refuses to hear them, tell it to the church. But if he refuses even to hear the church, let him be to you like a heathen and a tax collector. Assuredly, I say to you, whatever you bind on earth will be bound in heaven, and whatever you loose on earth will be loosed in heaven" (Matt. 18:15-18).

"In dealing with erring church members, God's people are carefully to follow the instruction given by the Savior in the eighteenth chapter of Matthew.

"Human beings are Christ's property, purchased by Him at an infinite price, bound to Him by the love that He and His Father have manifested for them. How careful, then, we should be in our dealing with one another! Men have no right to surmise evil in regard to their fellow men. Church members have no right to follow their own impulses and inclinations in dealing with fellow members who have erred. They should not even express their prejudices regarding the erring, for thus they place in other minds the leaven of evil. . . .

" 'If thy brother shall trespass against thee,' Christ declared, 'go and tell him his fault between thee and him alone.' . . . Do not tell others of the wrong. One person is told, then another, and still another; and continually the report grows, and the evil increases, till the whole church is made to suffer. Settle the matter 'between thee and him alone.' This is God's plan."—7T 260.

God's Plan—"Whatever the character of the offense, this does not change the plan that God has made for the settlement of misunderstandings and personal injuries. Speaking alone and in the spirit of Christ to the one who is in fault will often remove the difficulty. Go to the erring one, with a heart filled with Christ's love and sympathy, and seek to adjust the matter. Reason with him calmly and quietly. Let no angry words escape your lips. Speak in a way that will appeal to his better judgment. Remember the words: 'He which converteth the sinner from the error of his way shall save a soul from death, and shall hide a multitude of sins.' James 5:20. . . .

"All heaven is interested in the interview between the one who has been injured and the one who is in error. As the erring one accepts the reproof offered in the love of Christ, and acknowledges his wrong, asking forgiveness from God and from his brother, the sunshine of heaven fills his heart. . . . The Spirit of God binds heart to heart, and there is music in heaven over the union brought about. . . .

" 'But if he will not hear thee, then take with thee one or two more, that in the mouth of two or three witnesses every word may be established.'. . . Take with you those who are spiritually minded, and talk with the one in error in regard to the wrong. . . . As he sees their agreement in the matter, his mind may be enlightened.

" 'And if he shall neglect to hear them,' what then shall be done? Shall a few persons in a board meeting take upon themselves the responsibility of disfellowshiping the erring one? 'If he shall neglect to hear them, tell it unto the church.' . . . Let the church take action in regard to its members.

" 'But if he neglect to hear the church, let him be unto thee as an heathen man and a publican.' . . . If he will not heed the voice of the church, if he refuses all the efforts made to reclaim him, upon the church rests the responsibility of separating him from fellowship. His name should then be stricken from the books.

"No church officer should advise, no committee should recommend, nor should any church vote, that the name of a wrongdoer shall be removed from the church books, until the instruction given by Christ has been faithfully followed. When this instruction has been followed, the church has cleared herself before God. The evil must then be made to appear as it is, and must be removed, that it may not become more and more widespread. The health and purity of the church must be preserved, that she may stand before God unsullied, clad in the robes of Christ's righteousness. . . .

" 'Verily I say unto you,' Christ continued, 'whatsoever ye shall bind on earth shall be bound in heaven: and whatsoever ye shall loose on earth shall be loosed in heaven.' . . .

"This statement holds its force in all ages. On the church has been conferred the power to act in Christ's stead. It is God's instrumentality for the preservation of order and discipline among His people. To it the Lord has delegated the power to settle all questions respecting its prosperity, purity, and order. Upon it rests the responsibility of excluding from its fellowship those who are unworthy, who by their un-Christlike conduct would bring dishonor on the truth. Whatever the church does that is in accordance with the directions given in God's Word will be ratified in heaven."—7T 261-263.

Authority of the Church—"The world's Redeemer has invested great power with His church. He states the rules to be applied in cases of trial with its members. After He has given explicit directions as to the course to be pursued, He says: 'Verily I say unto you, Whatsoever ye shall bind on earth shall be bound in heaven: and whatsoever [in church discipline] ye shall loose on earth shall be loosed in heaven.' Thus even the heavenly authority ratifies the discipline of the church in regard to its members when the Bible rule has been followed.

"The Word of God does not give license for one man to set up his judgment in opposition to the judgment of the church, neither is he allowed to urge his opinions against the opinions of the church."—3T 428.

Church's Responsibility—"God holds His people, as a body, responsible for the sins existing in individuals among them. If the leaders of the church neglect to diligently search out the sins which bring the displeasure of God upon the body, they become responsible for these sins."—3T 269.

"If there were no church discipline and government, the church would go to fragments; it could not hold together as a body."—3T 428.

Unconsecrated Resist Discipline—"There are many who do not have the discretion of Joshua and who have no special duty to search out wrongs and to deal promptly with the sins existing among them. Let not such hinder those who have the burden of this work upon them; let them not stand in the way of those who have this duty to do. Some make it a point to question and doubt and find fault because others do the work that God has not laid upon them. These stand directly in the way to hinder those upon whom God has laid the burden of reproving and correcting prevailing sins in order that His frown may be turned away from His people. Should a case like Achan's be among us, there are many who would accuse those who might act the part of Joshua in searching out the wrong, of having a wicked, fault-finding spirit. God is not to be trifled with and His warnings disregarded with impunity by a perverse people. . . .

"Those who work in the fear of God to rid the church of hindrances and to correct grievous wrongs, that the people of God may see the necessity of abhorring sin and may prosper in purity, and that the name of God may be glorified, will ever meet with resisting influences from the unconsecrated."—3T 270, 271.

Safeguarding Unity of the Church—Christians should make every effort to avoid tendencies that would divide them and bring dishonor to their cause. "It is the purpose of God that His children shall blend in unity. Do they not expect to live together in the same heaven? . . . Those who refuse to work in harmony greatly dishonor God."—8T 240. The church should discourage actions that threaten harmony among its members and should consistently encourage unity.

Although all members have equal rights within the church, no individual member or group should start a movement or form an organization or seek to encourage a following for the attainment of any objective or for the teaching of any doctrine or message not in harmony with the fundamental religious objectives and teachings of the Church. Such a course would result in the fostering of a divisive spirit, the fragmenting of the witness of the Church, and thus in hindering of the Church's discharge of its obligations to the Lord and the world.

Reconciliation of Differences—Every effort should be made to settle differences among church members and contain the controversy within the smallest possible sphere. Reconciliation of differences within the church should, in most cases, be possible without recourse either to a conciliation process provided by the Church or to civil litigation.

"If matters of difficulty between brethren were not laid open before others, but frankly spoken of between themselves in the spirit of Christian love, how much evil might be prevented! How many roots of bitterness whereby many are defiled would be destroyed, and how closely and tenderly might the followers of Christ be united in His love!"—TMB 59. (See p. 58.)

"Contentions, strife, and lawsuits between brethren are a disgrace to the cause of truth. Those who take such a course expose the church to the ridicule of her enemies and cause the powers of darkness to triumph. They are piercing the wounds of Christ afresh and putting Him to an open shame. By ignoring the authority of the church they show contempt for God, who gave to the church its authority."—5T 242, 243.

Civil litigation is often carried on in a spirit of contention that results from and reveals human selfishness. It is this kind of adversarial proceedings that must be discouraged by a church that seeks to exhibit the spirit of Christ. Christian unselfishness will lead followers of Christ to suffer themselves to be defrauded (1 Cor. 6:7) rather than to "go to law before the unrighteous, and not before the saints" (1 Cor. 6:1).

While there are, in the modern world, occasions for seeking decrees of civil courts, Christians should prefer settlement within the authority of the Church and should limit the seeking of such decrees to cases that are clearly within the jurisdiction of the civil courts and not within the authority of the Church or for which the Church agrees it has no adequate process for orderly settlement. Such suits before civil courts should never become revengeful adversary proceedings but should develop out of a desire to seek arbitration and to settle differences amicably.

Examples of such civil cases may include, but are not limited to, the settlement of insurance claims, the issuance of decrees affecting the boundaries and ownership of real property, the deciding of some matters involving the administration of estates, and the awarding of custody of minor children.

While the Church should set up procedures within the constraints of legal practice to avoid the type of litigation referred to in 1 Corinthians 6, it should constantly be on guard against turning from its gospel mission and taking up the duties of a civil magistrate. (See Luke 12:13, 14 and 9T 216-218.)

God's ideal for members of His Church is that they should, as far as possible, "live peaceably with all men" (Rom. 12:18). The Church should use its readily accessible and reasonably prompt process by which many differences among members can be settled. Should the Church fail to respond to a request for help in reconciling a difference, or if the Church acknowledges that the nature of the case is such that it is not within its authority, it should be recognized that the member has exhausted the possibilities of the biblically outlined procedure for the settlement of differences and that what he/ she should do beyond that point is a matter for his/her conscience. (See *The SDA Bible Commentary*, vol. 6, p. 698.)

However, when the Church, endeavoring to assist in timely and amicable settlement of differences among its members, recommends a solution, members should not summarily reject the recommendation. As 1 Corinthians 6:7 indicates, it is no light matter for a member, outside the orderly processes of the Church, to litigate a grievance against another member.

Members who demonstrate impatience and selfishness by their unwillingness to wait for and accept recommendations of the Church in the settlement of grievances against other church members may properly be subject to the discipline of the church (see pp. 58, 59) because of the disruptive effect on the Church and their refusal to recognize properly constituted Church authority.

Settlement of Grievances of Members Against the Church—The same principles that influence resolution of differences among members apply to the settlement of grievances of members against Church organizations and institutions.

Members should not instigate litigation against any Church entity except under circumstances where the Church has not provided adequate process for orderly settlement of the grievance or where the nature of the case is such that it is clearly not within the authority of the Church to settle.

Settlement of Grievances of the Church Against Members—At times Church organizations or institutions may have grievances against members. In such circumstances, Church administrators must, in Christian forbearance, keep in mind the biblical counsel for settling disputes among Christians and apply that counsel to the settlement of grievances of the Church against its members. The Church should, in preference to litigating matters in a secular court, make every reasonable effort in cooperation with the member to provide a process by which orderly settlement of the problem can be accomplished.

The Church recognizes the need of exercising great care to protect the highest spiritual interests of its members, to ensure fair treatment, and to safeguard the name of the Church. It cannot afford to deal lightly with such sins or permit personal considerations to affect its actions, and at the same time it must strive to reclaim and restore those who err.

"If the erring one repents and submits to Christ's discipline, he is to be given another trial. And even if he does not repent, even if he stands outside the church, God's servants still have a work to do for him. They are to seek earnestly to win him to repentance. And, however aggravated may have been his offense, if he yields to the striving of the Holy Spirit and, by confessing and forsaking his sin, gives evidence of repentance, he is to be forgiven and welcomed to the fold again. His brethren are to encourage him in the right way, treating him as they would wish to be treated were they in his place, considering themselves lest they also be tempted."—7T 263.

Reasons for Discipline

The reasons for which members shall be subject to discipline are:

1.   Denial of faith in the fundamentals of the gospel and in the fundamental beliefs of the Church or teaching doctrines contrary to the same.

2.   Violation of the law of God, such as worship of idols, murder, stealing, profanity, gambling, Sabbathbreaking, and willful and habitual falsehood.

3.   Violation of the commandment of the law of God, which reads, "You shall not commit adultery" (Ex. 20:14, Matt. 5:27-28), as it relates to the marriage institution and the Christian home, biblical standards of moral conduct, and any act of sexual intimacy outside of a marriage relationship and/or non-consensual acts of sexual conduct within a marriage, whether those acts are legal or illegal. Such acts include but are not limited to child sexual abuse, including abuse of the vulnerable. Marriage is defined as a public, lawfully binding, monogamous, heterosexual relationship between one man and one woman.

4.   Fornication, which includes among other issues, promiscuity, homosexual activity, incest, sodomy, and bestiality.

5.   The production, use, or distribution of pornographic material.

6.   Remarriage of a divorced person, except the spouse who has remained faithful to the marriage vow in a divorce for adultery or for sexual perversions.

7.   Physical violence, including violence within the family.

8.   Fraud or willful misrepresentation in business.

9.   Disorderly conduct which brings reproach upon the church.

10.   Adherence to or taking part in a divisive or disloyal movement or organization. (See p. 59.)

11.   Persistent refusal to recognize properly constituted church authority or to submit to the order and discipline of the church.

12.   The use, manufacture, or sale of alcoholic beverages.

13.   The use, manufacture, or sale of tobacco in any of its forms for human consumption.

14.   The use or manufacture of illicit drugs or the use, misuse, or sale of narcotics or drugs without appropriate medical cause and license.

Process of Discipline

When grievous sins are involved, the church has two ways in which disciplinary measures must be taken:
1. By a vote of censure.
2. By a vote to remove from membership.

Discipline by Censure—In cases where the offense is not considered by the church to be so serious as to warrant the extreme course of removing membership, the church may express its disapproval by a vote of censure.

Censure has two purposes: (1) To enable the church to express its disapproval of a grievous offense that has brought disgrace upon the cause of God and (2) to impress offending members with the need for a change of life and reformation of conduct and to give them a period of grace and probation during which to make those changes.

A vote of censure is for a stated period of from a minimum of one month to a maximum of 12 months. It terminates an erring member's election or appointment to all offices and removes the privilege of election while it is in effect. Members under censure have no right to participate by voice or by vote in the affairs of the church or lead church activities, such as teaching a Sabbath School class. They are not deprived, however, of the privilege of sharing the blessings of Sabbath School, church worship, or communion. Membership may not be transferred during the period of censure.

Votes of censure must not carry any provision involving removal of membership in case of failure to comply with any condition imposed. Assessment should be made at the expiration of the period of censure to determine whether the disciplined members have changed course. If their conduct is satisfactory, they may then be considered in regular standing without further action and shall be notified that the censure has ended. If their conduct is not satisfactory, the church again should consider appropriate discipline. Any return to church office must be by election.

Discipline by Removal From Membership—Removing individuals from membership in the church, the body of Christ, is the ultimate discipline that the church can administer. Only after the instruction given in this chapter has been followed, after counsel from the pastor or the conference when the pastor is unavailable, and after all possible efforts have been made to win and restore them to right paths, should an individual be removed from membership.

No Additional Tests of Fellowship—No minister, congregation, or conference has authority to establish tests of fellowship. This authority rests with the General Conference Session. Anyone seeking to apply tests other than those herein set forth does not, therefore, properly represent the Church. (See 1T 207.)

Timeliness of Discipline—The church must care for the disciplinary process within a reasonable time and then communicate its decisions with kindness and promptness. Delay in administering discipline may increase the frustration and suffering of the member and the church itself.

Caution About Judging Character and Motive—"Christ has plainly taught that those who persist in open sin must be separated from the church, but He has not committed to us the work of judging character and motive. He knows our nature too well to entrust this work to us. Should we try to uproot from the church those whom we suppose to be spurious Christians, we should be sure to make mistakes. Often we regard as hopeless subjects the very ones whom Christ is drawing to Himself. Were we to deal with these souls according to our imperfect judgment, it would perhaps extinguish their last hope. Many who think themselves Christians will at last be found wanting. Many will be in heaven who their neighbors supposed would never enter there. Man judges from appearance, but God judges the heart. The tares and the wheat are to grow together until the harvest; and the harvest is the end of probationary time. There is in the Savior's words another lesson, a lesson of wonderful forbearance and tender love. As the tares have their roots closely intertwined with those of the good grain, so false brethren in the church may be closely linked with true disciples. The real character of these pretended believers is not fully manifested. Were they to be separated from the church, others might be caused to stumble, who but for this would have remained steadfast."—COL 71, 72.

At a Properly Called Meeting—Members may be disciplined for sufficient cause, but only at a properly called business meeting (see p. 128) after the church board has reviewed the case. The meeting must be presided over by an ordained pastor, or licensed pastor who is ordained as a local elder of the church concerned, or, in the pastor's absence and in counsel with the pastor or with the conference president, an elder of the local church.

By Majority Vote—Members may be removed from membership or otherwise disciplined only by a majority vote of members present and voting at a duly called meeting. "The majority of the church is a power which should control its individual members."—5T 107.

Church Board Cannot Remove Members—The board may recommend to a business meeting the removal of members, but under no circumstance does the board have the right to take final action. Except in the case of the death of members, the clerk can remove a name from the records only after a vote of the church in a business meeting.

Fundamental Rights of the Members—Members have a fundamental right to prior notification of the disciplinary meeting and the right to be heard in their own defense, introduce evidence, and produce witnesses. No church should vote to discipline a member under circumstances that deprive the member of these rights. Written notice must be given at least two weeks before the meeting and include the reasons for the disciplinary hearing.

Lawyers Not to Represent Members—The work of the Church in its administration of order and discipline is an ecclesiastical function that in no sense has to do with civil or legal procedure. Therefore, the Church does not recognize the right of members to bring legal counsel to represent them in any meeting called to administer order or discipline or for the transaction of any other church business. Members wanting to bring legal counsel into a meeting should be informed that they will not be given a hearing if they insist on bringing legal counsel.

The church also should exclude all nonmembers from any church meeting called for the administration of church order or discipline, except when they are called as witnesses.

Transferring Members Under Censure—No church shall receive into membership persons who are under censure of another congregation, because that would condone the offenses for which the members have been disciplined. The acceptance into membership of those under discipline is such a serious violation of Church policy that an offending church may be subject to discipline by the conference constituency.

Members Not to Be Removed for Nonattendance—Church leaders should faithfully visit absentee members and encourage them to resume attendance and to enjoy the blessings of worship with the congregation.

When because of age, infirmity, or other unavoidable cause members find it impossible to attend worship services regularly, they should keep in contact with church leaders by letter or other means. However, as long as members are loyal to the doctrines of the Church, nonattendance shall not be considered sufficient cause for removal from membership.

Members Moving Away and Not Reporting—When members move, they should inform the clerk or elder of their new address. While remaining members of that church, they should report and send their tithe and offerings at least quarterly. If, however, members move without leaving a forwarding address and make no effort to contact or report to the church, and the church cannot locate them for at least two years, then the church may certify that it has tried without success to locate the members and the members may be removed by a vote of the church. The clerk should record in the membership record: "Whereabouts unknown. Voted to designate as missing."

Members Not to Be Removed for Pecuniary Reasons—Though members should support the work of the Church to the extent they are able, they should never be removed because of their inability or failure to contribute financially to the Church.

Removing Members at Their Request—Great care should be exercised in dealing with members who request to be removed from membership.

The Church recognizes the right of the individual to withdraw membership. Letters of resignation shall be presented to the board, where the resignation will be recorded with the effective date according to the resignation letter. Out of Christian consideration for the individuals involved, action shall be taken without public discussion. Efforts should be made to restore the individual to the church family.

Notification to Those Removed From Membership—A church removing members must notify them in writing of the action taken but with the assurance of enduring spiritual interest and personal concern. This communication should, where possible, be delivered in person by the pastor or by a board designee. The former members should be assured that the church hopes they will return to the church and that one day there will be eternal fellowship together in the kingdom of God.

Reinstating Those Previously Removed From Membership

When persons have been removed for discipline, the church should, where possible, maintain contact and manifest the spirit of friendship and love, endeavoring to bring them back to the Lord.

Those previously removed may be received again into membership when confession of wrongs committed is made, evidence is given of real repentance and change of life, and the life is consistent with Church standards and it is clear that the member will fully submit to Church order and discipline. Such reinstatement should preferably be in the church from which the member was dismissed. However, when this is not possible, the church where the person is requesting reinstatement must seek information from the former church about the reasons for which the person was removed from membership.

When dealing with perpetrators of sexual abuse, it should be remembered that restoration to membership does not remove all consequences of such a serious violation. While attendance at church activities may be permissible with properly established guidelines, a person convicted or disciplined for sexual abuse should not be placed in a role which could put them in contact with children, youth, and other vulnerable individuals. Neither shall they be given any position which would encourage vulnerable individuals to trust them implicitly.

Because removal from membership is the most serious form of discipline, the period of time before members may be reinstated should be sufficient to demonstrate that the issues which led to removal from membership have been resolved beyond reasonable doubt. It is expected that readmission to membership will be done in connection with rebaptism.

Right of Appeal for Reinstatement

Right of Appeal for Reinstatement—While it is the right of the church to administer discipline, this does not set aside the rights of members to seek fairness. If members believe that they have been treated unfairly by the local church, or not had the right to be heard fairly, and the church is unwilling to reconsider the case or if the officers refuse to consider their applications for reinstatement, the former members have a right to appeal in writing to the church for a hearing. The church should not neglect or refuse to grant such hearings. If it does, or if the former members still feel unfairly treated by the church after the appeal, they have the right to a final appeal for a hearing to the executive committee of the conference.

If, after a full and impartial hearing, the conference committee is satisfied that an injustice has been inflicted by the church, the committee may recommend reinstatement to membership. But if membership is still refused by the church, then the conference committee may recommend membership in some other church. On the other hand, if it finds good grounds for sustaining the church in refusing to reinstate the former members, it will so record its decision.

CHAPTER 8

Local Church Officers and Organizations

Choosing quality officers is important for the prosperity of the church, which should exercise the greatest care when calling men and women into positions of sacred responsibility.

General Qualifications

Moral and Religious Fitness—"Moreover you shall select from all the people able men, such as fear God, men of truth, hating covetousness; and place such over them to be rulers of thousands, rulers of hundreds, rulers of fifties, and rulers of tens" (Ex. 18:21).

"Therefore, brethren, seek out from among you seven men of good reputation, full of the Holy Spirit and wisdom, whom we may appoint over this business" (Acts 6:3).

"Moreover he must have a good testimony among those who are outside, lest he fall into reproach and the snare of the devil" (1 Tim. 3:7).

"And the things that you have heard from me among many witnesses, commit these to faithful men who will be able to teach others also" (2 Tim. 2:2).

"A bishop [elder] then must be blameless, the husband of one wife, temperate, sober-minded, of good behavior, hospitable, able to teach; not given to wine, not violent, not greedy for money, but gentle, not quarrelsome, not covetous; one who rules his own house well, having his children in submission with all reverence (for if a man does not know how to rule his own house, how will he take care of the church of God?); not a novice, lest being puffed up with pride he fall into the same condemnation as the devil. Moreover he must have a good testimony among those who are outside, lest he fall into reproach and the snare of the devil.

"Likewise deacons must be reverent, not double-tongued, not given to much wine, not greedy for money, holding the mystery of the faith with a pure conscience. But let these also first be tested; then let them serve as deacons, being found blameless. Likewise, their wives must be reverent, not slanderers, temperate, faithful in all things. Let deacons be the husbands of one wife, ruling their children and their own houses well. For those who have served well as deacons obtain for themselves a good standing and great boldness in the faith which is in Christ Jesus" (1 Tim. 3:2-13; see also Titus 1:5-11 and 2:1, 7, 8).

"Let no one despise your youth, but be an example to the believers in word, in conduct, in love, in spirit, in faith, in purity. Till I come, give attention to reading, to exhortation, to doctrine. . . . Take heed to yourself and to the doctrine. Continue in them, for in doing this you will save both yourself and those who hear you" (1 Tim. 4:12-16).

Feeding and Guarding the Church—The apostle Paul called together "the elders of the church" and counseled them: "Therefore take heed to yourselves and to all the flock, among which the Holy Spirit has made you overseers, to shepherd the church of God which He purchased with His own blood. For I know this, that after my departure savage wolves will come in among you, not sparing the flock. Also from among yourselves men will rise up, speaking perverse things, to draw away the disciples after themselves. Therefore watch, and remember that for three years I did not cease to warn everyone night and day with tears" (Acts 20:17, 28-31; see also 1 Peter 5:1-3).

Respecting Pastors and Officers—"And we urge you, brethren, to recognize those who labor among you, and are over you in the Lord and admonish you, and to esteem them very highly in love for their work's sake. Be at peace among yourselves" (1 Thess. 5:12, 13; see also 1 Tim. 5:17 and Heb. 13:7, 17).

"The Thessalonian believers were greatly annoyed by men coming among them with fanatical ideas and doctrines. Some were 'disorderly, working not at all, but . . . busybodies.' The church had been properly organized, and officers had been appointed to act as ministers and deacons. But there were some, self-willed and impetuous, who refused to be subordinate to those who held positions of authority in the church. They claimed not only the right of private judgment, but that of publicly urging their views upon the church. In view of this, Paul called the attention of the Thessalonians to the respect and deference due to those who had been chosen to occupy positions of authority in the church."—AA 261, 262.

"Those who hold responsible positions in the church may have faults in common with other people and may err in their decisions; but notwithstanding this, the church of Christ on earth has given to them an authority that cannot be lightly esteemed."—4T 17.

Not Hurried Into Office—"In many places we meet men who have been hurried into responsible positions as elders of the church when they are not qualified for such a position. They have not proper government over themselves. Their influence is not good. The church is in trouble continually in consequence of the defective character of the leader. Hands have been laid too suddenly upon these men."—4T 406, 407. (See also 5T 617 and 1 Tim. 5:22.)

Those Opposing Unity Not Suitable for Office—"There have of late arisen among us men who profess to be the servants of Christ, but whose work is opposed to that unity which our Lord established in the church. They have original plans and methods of labor. They desire to introduce changes into the church to suit their ideas of progress and imagine that grand results are thus to be secured. These men need to be learners rather than teachers in the school of Christ. They are ever restless, aspiring to accomplish some great work, to do something that will bring honor to themselves. They need to learn that most profitable of all lessons, humility and faith in Jesus. . . .

"Teachers of the truth, missionaries, officers in the church, can do a good work for the Master if they will but purify their own souls by obeying the truth."—5T 238.

Unsafe to Choose Those Refusing to Cooperate—"God has placed in the church, as His appointed helpers, men of varied talents, that through the combined wisdom of many the mind of the Spirit may be met. Men who move in accordance with their own strong traits of character, refusing to yoke up with others who have had a long experience in the work of God, will become blinded by self-confidence, unable to discern between the false and the true. It is not safe for such ones to be chosen as leaders in the church; for they would follow their own judgment and plans, regardless of the judgment of their brethren. It is easy for the enemy to work through those who, themselves needing counsel at every step, undertake the guardianship of souls in their own strength, without having learned the lowliness of Christ."—AA 279. (See pp. 33, 34, 118-121.)

Local Membership—Members in regular standing are eligible for election to leadership positions in the church where they hold membership. (See pp. 110-113.) Exceptions may be made for the following:

1.   Students who are members in regular standing but who, for purposes of education, live away from home and regularly attend a church in the area of their temporary residence.

2.   A conference employee assigned by the conference as pastor/leader for two or more congregations. (See pp. 114, 115.)

3.   An elder who, when necessary and with the recommendation of the conference committee, may be elected to serve in more than one church within a district. (See p. 74.)

Other exceptions may be considered by the conference committee.

Setting Tithing Example—All officers shall set an example in the matter of returning a faithful tithe to the Church. Anyone who fails to set such an example shall not be elected to church office.

Not Delegates Ex Officio—No church officer is a delegate ex officio to a conference session. If the church wants an officer to serve as a delegate, it must elect that officer as a delegate.

Distributing Responsibility—The church should not lay too much responsibility on a small group of willing officers, while others are underused. Unless circumstances make it necessary, election of one individual to several offices should be discouraged.

Removal and Readmission—When an officer is removed from membership and subsequently readmitted, the readmittance does not reinstate the individual to the former office.

Term of Office

The term of office for officers of both the church and its auxiliary organizations shall be one year, except where the church in a business meeting votes to have elections every two years in order to facilitate continuity and development of spiritual gifts and eliminate the work involved in having yearly elections.

While it is not advisable for one person to serve indefinitely in a particular position, officers may be reelected.

Elders

Religious Leaders of the Church—Elders must be recognized by the church as strong spiritual leaders and must have good reputations both in the church and community. In the absence of a pastor, elders are the spiritual leaders of the church and by precept and example must seek to lead the church into a deeper and fuller Christian experience.

Elders should be able to conduct the services of the church and minister in both word and doctrine when the assigned pastor is unavailable. However, elders should not be chosen primarily because of social position or speaking ability, but because of their consecrated lives and leadership abilities.

Elders may be reelected, but it is not advisable for them to serve indefinitely. The church is under no obligation to reelect and may choose others whenever changes seem advisable. Upon the election of new elders, the former elders no longer function as elders but may be elected to other church offices.

Ordination of Elders—Election to the office of elder does not in itself qualify one as an elder. Ordination is required before an elder has authority to function. Between election and ordination, the elected elder may function as church leader but not administer the ordinances of the church.

The ordination service is performed only by an ordained pastor currently credentialed by the conference. As a courtesy, a visiting ordained pastor may be invited to assist. However, only on the specific request of conference officers would a visiting ordained pastor or a retired ordained pastor conduct the ordination.

The sacred rite of ordination should be simply performed in the presence of the church and may include a brief outline of the office of elder, the qualities required, and the principal duties the elder will be authorized to perform. After the exhortation, the ordained pastor, assisted by other ordained pastors and/or local elders who are participating in the service, will ordain the elders by prayer and the laying on of hands. (See p. 37.)

Once ordained, elders need not be ordained again if reelected, or upon election as elders of other churches, provided they have maintained regular membership status. They are also qualified to serve as deacons.

Relationship to the Pastor—If the conference committee assigns a pastor or pastors to the congregation, the pastor, or senior pastor if more than one, should be considered the ranking officer and the local elders as assistants. Since their work is closely related, they should work together harmoniously. The pastor should not assume all lines of responsibility, but should share these with the elders and other officers. The pastor regularly serving the church acts as the chairperson of the board. (See pp. 32, 131.) There may be circumstances, however, when it would be advisable for an elder to act as chairperson. The pastoral work of the church should be shared by the pastor and the elders. In counsel with the pastor, the elders should visit members, minister to the sick, foster prayer ministries, arrange or lead out in anointing services and child dedications, encourage the disheartened, and assist in other pastoral responsibilities. As undershepherds, elders should exercise constant vigilance over the flock.

If the pastor is a licensed minister, the church or churches served should elect the pastor as an elder. (See p. 33.)

Because the pastor is appointed to the position in the church by the conference, the pastor serves the church as a conference employee, is responsible to the conference committee, and maintains a sympathetic and cooperative relation to and works in harmony with all the plans and policies of the local church. Elders, who are elected by the church, are responsible to that body and to its board. (See below.)

Work of Elders Is Local—The authority and work of elders are confined to the church in which their election has been made. It is not permissible for a conference committee by vote to confer on an elder the status that is granted to an ordained pastor to serve other churches as elder. If that need exists, the conference committee may recommend to the church needing an elder that it invite and elect the elder of a nearby church to serve. Thus by election one individual may, when necessary, serve more than one church. Such an arrangement should be made only in counsel with the conference committee. Authority to elect elders is inherent in the local church and not in the conference committee. The only way one may be qualified for serving the Church at large is by ordination to the gospel ministry. (See pp. 32, 73, 74.)

Conducting Church Services—Under the pastor, or in the absence of the pastor, an elder is responsible for the services of the church and must either conduct them or arrange for someone to do so. Communion services must always be conducted by an ordained/commissioned pastor or local elder. The pastor usually chairs the business meeting. In the absence of the pastor, and with approval of the pastor or the conference president, an elder should serve as chairperson.

Baptismal Service—In the absence of an ordained pastor, an elder shall request the conference president to arrange for the baptism of those desiring to unite with the church. (See pp. 45-49.) An elder should not officiate in the service without first obtaining permission from the conference president.

Marriage Ceremony—In a marriage ceremony the charge, vows, and declaration of marriage are given only by an ordained pastor except in those areas where division committees have approved that selected licensed or commissioned pastors who have been ordained as local elders may perform the ceremony. (See p. 33.) Local laws may require that persons conducting marriage ceremonies also hold state licensure/permit to do so. An ordained pastor, a licensed or commissioned pastor, or an elder may deliver the sermonette, offer the prayer, and give the blessing. (See Notes, #1, p. 173.)

To Foster Tithing—By faithfully returning tithe, elders do much to encourage other members to return a faithful tithe. (See pp. 136, 137, 169.) Elders can foster tithing by public presentation of the scriptural privilege and responsibility of stewardship and by personal labor with members in a tactful and helpful manner.

Elders should regard all financial matters pertaining to members as confidential and shall not give such information to unauthorized persons.

To Foster Bible Study, Prayer, and a Relationship With Jesus— As spiritual leaders, elders are responsible for encouraging members to develop a personal relationship with Jesus by strengthening their habits of personal Bible study and prayer. Elders should model a commitment to Bible study and prayer. An effective personal prayer life of every member, supporting all ministries and programs of the local church, will enhance the church's mission. Elders may ask the board to appoint a council to assist in this role of development and encouragement.

To Foster All Lines of Work—Under and in cooperation with the pastor, elders are spiritual leaders of the church and are responsible for fostering all departments and activities of the work. Elders should maintain a mutually helpful relationship with other officers.

To Cooperate With the Conference—The pastor, elders, and all officers should cooperate with conference officers and departmental directors in carrying out approved plans. They should inform the church of all regular and special offerings, promote all the programs and activities of the church, and encourage all officers to support conference plans and policies.

Elders should work closely with the treasurer and see that all conference funds are remitted promptly to the conference treasurer at the time established by the conference. Elders should see that the clerk's report is sent promptly to the conference secretary at the close of each quarter.

Elders should regard all correspondence from the conference office as important. Letters calling for announcements should be presented at the proper time.

In the absence of the pastor, the first elder (see p. 114) should see that the church elects delegates to conference sessions and that the clerk sends the names of delegates to the conference office.

To Foster Worldwide Work—Elders also should foster world mission work by carefully studying the worldwide work and encouraging members to personally support mission work. Their kindly, tactful attitude will encourage liberality of members both in church services and Sabbath School.

Training and Equipping of Elders—The Ministerial Association, in cooperation with the departments, promotes the training and equipping of elders. However, the pastor has the primary responsibility for training elders. (See Notes, #2, p. 173.)

Free to Work Effectively—Elders especially should be left free of other burdens to perform effectively their many duties. It may be advisable in some cases to ask elders to lead the outreach (missionary) work of the church, but even this should be avoided if other talent is available.

First Elder—It may be advisable, because of church size, to choose more than one elder because the burdens of the office are too great for one person. If the church elects more than one elder, one should be designated "first elder." The work should be divided among the elders in harmony with their experience and ability.

Limitation of Authority—Elders do not have the authority to receive or remove members. This is done only by vote of the church. Only the board may recommend that the church vote to receive or remove members. (See pp. 48, 53, 54.)

Church Leaders

Occasionally no one possesses the experience and qualifications to serve as an elder. Under such circumstances the church should elect a person to be known as "leader." In the absence of the pastor or a conference-assigned pastor, the leader is responsible for the services of the church, including business meetings. The leader must either conduct the church service or arrange for someone else to do so. If the church leader is unable to lead out in the business meeting, the conference should be contacted for assistance.

A leader, who is not an ordained elder, may not administer baptism, conduct the Lord's Supper, perform the marriage ceremony, or preside at business meetings when members are disciplined. A request should be made to the conference president for an ordained pastor to preside at such meetings.

Deacons

The New Testament identifies the office of deacon with the Greek word *diakonos*, from which the English "deacon" is derived. The Greek word is variously interpreted as "servant, minister, writer, attendant" and in Christian circles has acquired the specialized meaning now attached to "deacon."

The men who came to be known as the seven deacons of the apostolic church were chosen and ordained to attend to the business of the church. (See Acts 6:1-8.) Their qualifications, slightly less exacting than those of elders, are listed in 1 Timothy 3:8-13.

"The fact that these brethren had been ordained for the special work of looking after the needs of the poor did not exclude them from teaching the faith. On the contrary, they were fully qualified to instruct others in the truth, and they engaged in the work with great earnestness and success."—AA 90.

"The appointment of the seven to take the oversight of special lines of work proved a great blessing to the church. These officers gave careful consideration to individual needs as well as to the general financial interests of the church, and by their prudent management and their godly example they were an important aid to their fellow officers in binding together the various interests of the church into a united whole."—AA 89.

Today appointment of deacons through election brings similar blessings in church administration by relieving pastors, elders, and other officers of duties that deacons may perform well.

"The time and strength of those who in the providence of God have been placed in leading positions of responsibility in the church should be spent in dealing with the weightier matters demanding special wisdom and largeness of heart. It is not in the order of God that such men should be appealed to for the adjustment of minor matters that others are well qualified to handle."—AA 93.

The Ministerial Association, in connection with the departments, promotes the training and equipping of deacons. However, the pastor, in conjunction with the elder(s), has the primary responsibility for training the deacons. (See Notes, #3, p. 173)

Board of Deacons—Where a church has a number of deacons, it should organize a board of deacons chaired by the head deacon and with another deacon serving as secretary. Such a body provides a way to distribute responsibility and coordinate their contributions to the well-being of the congregation. It also provides a training ground where new deacons are instructed in their duties.

Deacons Must Be Ordained—Newly elected deacons cannot fill their office until they have been ordained by an ordained pastor currently credentialed by the conference.

The sacred rite of ordination should be characterized by simplicity and performed in the presence of the church. The pastor may give a brief outline of the biblical office of deacon, the qualities required for service, and the principal duties deacons are authorized to perform. After a short exhortation to faithfulness in service, the pastor, assisted by an elder where appropriate, ordains the deacons by prayer and the laying on of hands. (See p. 37.)

If they retain church membership, deacons, once ordained, do not have to be ordained again if they move their memberships to other churches. When the term for which they were elected expires, they must be reelected if they are to continue to serve as deacons.

Elders subsequently elected as deacons need not be ordained as deacons because ordination as elder covers this office.

Deacons Not Authorized to Preside— Deacons are not authorized to preside at the Lord's Supper, baptism, or business meetings and are not permitted to perform the marriage ceremony or officiate at the reception or transfer of members.

If a church has no one authorized to perform such duties, the church leader shall contact the conference for assistance.

Duties of Deacons—The work of deacons involves a wide range of services for the church, including:

1. *Assistance at Services and Meetings*—Deacons are usually responsible for welcoming members and visitors as they enter the church and for assisting them, where necessary, to find seats. They also cooperate with the pastor and elders for smooth functioning of all meetings.

2. *Visitation of Members*—In many churches visitation is arranged by distributing membership by districts and assigning a deacon to each district with the expectation that he will visit each home at least once a quarter.

3. *Preparation for Baptismal Services*—Deacons make necessary preparations for baptismal services. (See p. 48.)

4. *Assistance at Communion Service*— At the service of foot-washing, the deacons or deaconesses provide everything needed, such as towels, basins, water, and buckets. After the service they see that the utensils and linen are washed and properly stored.

Remaining bread and wine should not be consumed, but disposed of in a respectful manner by deacons and deaconesses following the Lord's Supper.

5. *Care of the Sick and Aiding the Poor and Unfortunate*—Deacons and deaconesses are charged with assisting the sick, poor, and unfortunate and should keep the church informed of their needs and enlist the support of members. Money should be provided for this work from the fund for the poor and needy. The treasurer, on recommendation from the board, will pass over to the deacons or deaconesses whatever may be needed for use in needy cases.

6. *Care and Maintenance of Property*—In churches where the responsibility for the care and maintenance of church property is not assigned to a building committee, deacons and deaconesses have this responsibility. (See Notes, #3, p. 173.)

Deaconesses

Deaconesses were included in the official staff of the early Christian churches.

"I commend to you Phoebe our sister, who is a servant of the church [deaconess] in Cenchrea, that you may receive her in the Lord in a manner worthy of the saints, and assist her in whatever business she has need of you; for indeed she has been a helper of many and of myself also" (Rom. 16:1, 2).

Deaconesses should be chosen for their consecration and other qualifications that fit them for the duties of the office.

The Ministerial Association, in connection with the departments, promotes the training and equipping of deaconesses. However, the pastor, in conjunction with the elder(s), has the primary responsibility for training the deaconesses. (See Notes, #3, p. 173)

Board of Deaconesses—If a church elects several deaconesses, it should organize a board of deaconesses chaired by the head deaconess and another deaconess serving as secretary. This board is authorized to assign duties to individual deaconesses and cooperates closely with the board of deacons, especially in welcoming members and visitors and in home visitation. (See p. 78.) It also provides a training ground where new deaconesses are instructed in their duties.

Ordination Service for Deaconesses—Such a service, like the ordination of deacons, would be carried out by an ordained pastor currently credentialed by the conference. The ordination service should be characterized by simplicity and performed in the presence of the church.

If they retain church membership, deaconesses do not have to be ordained again if they move their memberships to other churches. When the term for which they were elected expires, they must be reelected if they are to continue to serve as deaconesses.

Deaconesses Not Authorized to Preside—Deaconesses are not authorized to preside at any of the services of the church or business meetings and cannot perform the marriage ceremony or officiate at the reception or transfer of members.

If a church has no one authorized to perform such duties, the church leader shall contact the conference for assistance.

Duties of Deaconesses—Deaconesses serve the church in a wide variety of activities, including:

1. *Greeting and Visiting Guests and Members*—In many churches, deaconesses assist in greeting guests and members at meetings and in visiting members in their homes when they cannot attend services.

2. *Assistance at Baptisms*—Deaconesses ensure that female candidates are cared for both before and after the ceremony. They also give such counsel and help as may be necessary regarding suitable garments for baptism. Robes of suitable material should be provided. Where robes are used, the deaconesses should see that they are laundered and carefully stored. (See p. 48.)

3. *Arrangements for the Communion Service*—Deaconesses and deacons arrange for everything needed for this service and see that everything used is cared for afterward. (See p. 126.)

Before the communion service begins, deaconesses set the communion table, including preparing the bread and wine, pouring the wine, placing the plates of unleavened bread, and covering the table with the linen provided for that purpose.

Deaconesses assist in the service of foot-washing, giving special aid to women visitors and new members.

4. *The Care of the Sick and the Poor*—Deaconesses assist deacons in caring for the sick, needy, and unfortunate. (See p. 79.)

5. *Care and Maintenance of Property*—In churches where the responsibility for the care and maintenance of church property is not assigned to a building committee, deacons and deaconesses have this responsibility. (See Notes, #4, pp. 173-174.)

Clerk

Much of the efficient functioning of the church depends on the work of the clerk. Because of the important and specialized functions of this office, it is wise to choose one who can be reelected to provide continuity in record keeping and reporting. Large churches may elect assistant clerks as needed. When the clerk, as secretary, cannot attend a business meeting, the clerk should arrange for an assistant to be present to take the minutes. (See Notes, #5, p. 174.)

No Names Added or Removed Without Vote—The clerk has no authority to add names to or remove names from the membership record without a vote of the church, which must always vote to add or remove a name, except in the case of the death of a member, or when a member requests in writing to be removed from membership. When a member dies, the clerk will record the date of the death in the membership record. (See p. 55.)

When a member submits a written request to the church board to be removed from membership, the clerk will record the action of the board. (See pp. 66-67.)

Transferring Members—The clerk handles correspondence between members and churches in the transferring of memberships. (See pp. 51-55.)

Corresponding With Members—The clerk should try to keep in touch with absent members. (See Notes, #6, p. 174.)

Notice of Delegates for Conference Sessions—The clerk, on authorization of the board, promptly notifies the conference of delegates elected to represent the church at a conference session, using blanks or forms provided by the conference. (See p. 114.)

Reports to Be Furnished Promptly—The clerk must promptly furnish reports requested by the conference. Some are quarterly, others annual. It is essential that reports be sent to the conference secretary within the time specified because they are important for the accuracy of reports prepared by other organizations of the world Church. The clerk collects information for these reports from the other officers and department leaders.

Church Records—The clerk keeps church records, which should be carefully preserved. All records and account books of all officers are the property of the church and are to be surrendered to the newly elected clerk at the expiration of the term of office of the previous clerk, or to the church at any time during the term on request of the pastor or elders.

Treasurer

Because of the important functions of the treasurer, it is wise to choose one who can be reelected to provide continuity in record keeping and reporting. Large churches may elect assistant treasurers as needed.

The treasurer can greatly encourage faithfulness in the returning of tithe and deepen the spirit of liberality on the part of the members. A word of counsel given in the spirit of the Master will help members to render faithfully to God His own in tithes and offerings, even in a time of financial stringency.

Treasurer the Custodian of All Funds—The treasurer is the custodian of all church funds. These include (1) conference funds, (2) local church funds, and (3) funds belonging to auxiliary organizations of the local church.

All funds (conference, local church, and local church auxiliary) are deposited by the treasurer in a bank or financial institution account in the name of the church, unless the local conference authorizes another system.

Surplus church funds may be deposited in savings accounts upon authorization of the board. Where large balances are carried for building or special projects, the board may authorize separate bank accounts. Such accounts, however, shall be operated by the treasurer and reported to the church along with all other church funds.

All church bank accounts are exclusively for church funds and are never to be combined with any personal account or funds.

Conference Funds—Conference funds, which include tithe, all regular mission funds, and all funds for special conference projects and institutions, are trust funds. At the close of each month, or more often if requested by the conference, the treasurer shall send to the conference treasurer the entire amount of conference funds received during that period of time. The church may not borrow, use, or withhold such conference funds for any purpose.

Sabbath School Funds—All Sabbath School offerings are to be passed over weekly to the treasurer by the Sabbath School secretary-treasurer, the treasurer keeping a careful record of all such offerings. These mission funds are transmitted to the conference office as outlined in the previous paragraph. Sabbath School expense funds are held in trust, subject to the orders of the Sabbath School council (see pp. 97, 98), to meet the routine expenses of the Sabbath School.

Local Church Funds—Local church funds include church expense, building and repair funds, and the fund for the poor and needy. These funds belong to the local church and are disbursed by the treasurer only by authorization of the board or business meeting. However, the treasurer shall pay from the expense funds all bills for local expense that have been authorized by the board.

Funds of Auxiliary Organizations—Auxiliary organization funds include such funds as church outreach programs, family life, Adventist Youth Ministries, Adventist Community Services or Dorcas Society, Sabbath School expense, and that portion of the health ministries funds belonging to the church, and may include church school funds. All money received by and for these organizations is turned over promptly to the church treasurer by the secretary of the organization, the deacons, or whoever has received the funds. These funds belong to the auxiliary organizations of the church. They may be disbursed only by order of the auxiliary organization to which they belong.

The treasurer shall give receipts for all funds received. On receiving money from the treasurer, the secretary of the auxiliary organization shall give a proper receipt to the treasurer.

Safeguarding the Purpose of Funds—When an offering is taken for worldwide missions or for any general or local enterprise, all money placed in the offering plate (unless otherwise indicated by the donor) shall be counted as part of that particular offering. All offerings and gifts contributed by individuals for a specific fund or purpose must be used for that purpose. Neither the treasurer nor the board has the authority to divert any funds from the objective for which they were given.

The funds of auxiliary organizations, often donations given for specific purposes, are raised for that special part of the church's work for which the auxiliary organization is established. Such funds are held in trust by the treasurer, and they too may not be borrowed or in any way diverted by the treasurer or the board from the objective for which they were raised.

When an auxiliary organization is discontinued, the church in regular business session may take action indicating the disposition of any balance of funds in the account of the organization.

Money for Personal Literature Orders—Money for personal orders of literature, books, pamphlets, magazines, and subscriptions for periodicals is cared for by the treasurer in areas where a local Adventist Book Center does not exist. (See Notes, #7, p. 174.)

Proper Method for Payment of Money by Members—The treasurer should urge that all money paid in by members, other than the regular church collection, be placed in tithe and offering envelopes, unless an alternative method has been implemented by the conference. Members should list the various items and amounts on the envelope as indicated and to make sure that the money enclosed equals the total shown. They should also sign their names and give their addresses, and place the envelopes in the offering plate or hand them to the treasurer, who should preserve the envelopes to serve as vouchers until all accounts are checked by the conference auditor.

Members who return their tithes and offerings by check or postal notes should, where legally possible, make such checks or notes payable to the church, rather than to any individual.

Receipts to Members—Receipts should be issued promptly for all money received from members, no matter how small the amount, and a strict account of all receipts and payments should be kept by the treasurer. All general offerings not in envelopes should be counted by the treasurer in the presence of another officer, preferably a deacon or deaconess, and a receipt given to such officer.

Proper Method of Remitting Funds to the Conference—In sending remittances to the conference treasurer, all checks, bank drafts, or money orders should be made payable to the organization wherever legally possible and not to any individual. A copy of the treasurer's records for the period should be enclosed with the remittance. Remittance blanks are furnished by the conference. (See pp. 136, 137.)

Preservation of Financial Documents—Financial documents, vouchers, or receipted bills should be secured for all funds received and disbursed in accordance with the system authorized by the local conference.

Books Should Be Audited—The conference treasurer, or other individual appointed by the conference committee, audits the church financial records, usually each year.

The treasurer's books and other financial records relating to the work of the treasurer, the church school treasurer, and the treasurer of any other organization may be called for and inspected at any time by the conference auditor or by the pastor, district leader, head elder, or by any others authorized by the church board, but should not be made available to unauthorized persons. (See p. 141.)

Reports of all funds received and disbursed should be presented at the regular business meetings of the church. A copy of these reports should be given to the leading officers.

When the number of individuals returning tithe in the church is reported, the spouse and minor children who are non-wage earners but members of the church should be counted in this group, in addition to the wage earner of the family.

Relations With Members Confidential—The treasurer should always remember that relations with individual members are strictly confidential. The treasurer should never comment on the tithe returned by any member or on the income or anything concerning it, except to those who share the responsibility of the work. Great harm may be caused by failure to observe this rule.

Interest Coordinator

An interest coordinator should be elected to make sure that interests developed through the church's missionary outreach are cared for promptly. This person is a member of the board and the personal ministries council and works directly with the pastor and chairperson of that council.

Duties of this office include:

1. Keeping an organized list of all interests received by the church.

2. Assisting the pastor and chairperson of the personal ministries council in enlisting and recruiting qualified members for follow-up service.

3. Presenting to the board a monthly report on the number of interests received and followed up. When an interest is sufficiently developed, it should be shared with the pastor.

Departments and Other Organizations

Church structure, under the guidance of the Holy Spirit, is vital for the spiritual growth of members and for the fulfillment of the Church's mission. It is the skeleton of the ecclesiastical body. And "the whole body, joined and knit together by what every joint supplies, according to the effective working by which every part does its share, causes growth of the body for the edifying of itself in love" (Eph. 4:16).

The most important elements of structure and organization are the officers (see pp. 73-86) and the departments and other organizations. This section describes their objectives, leadership, and functions.

The work of the departments and auxiliary organizations is closely tied to the work of the pastor because all are equally engaged in gospel outreach. The pastor serves as a counselor to these organizations, and they in turn assist in the overall church outreach programs. In case of emergency, or where circumstances require, the pastor may call a meeting of any committee or organization.

Every church should utilize the services of the departments and organizations to nurture its members and accomplish the mission given by Christ (see Matt. 28:19; Rev. 10:11; 14:6).

Children's Ministries

Children's ministries develops the faith of children from birth through age 14, leading them into union with the Church. It seeks to provide multiple ministries that will lead children to Jesus and disciple them in their daily walk with Him. It cooperates with the Sabbath School and other departments to provide religious education to children and fulfills its mission by developing a variety of grace-oriented ministries for children that are inclusive, service-oriented, leadership-building, safe, and evangelistic.

"Too much importance cannot be placed on the early training of children. The lessons that the child learns during the first seven years of life have more to do with forming his character than all that it learns in future years."—CG 193.

"It is still true that children are the most susceptible to the teachings of the gospel; their hearts are open to divine influences, and strong to retain the lessons received. The little children may be Christians, having an experience in accordance with their years. They need to be educated in spiritual things, and parents should give them every advantage, that they may form characters after the similitude of the character of Christ."—DA 515.

"Children of eight, ten, or twelve years are old enough to be addressed on the subject of personal religion. . . . If properly instructed, very young children may have correct views of their state as sinners and of the way of salvation through Christ."—1T 400.

"When Jesus told the disciples not to forbid the children to come to Him, He was speaking to His followers in all ages—to officers of the church, to ministers, helpers, and all Christians. Jesus is drawing the children, and He bids us, Suffer them to come; as if He would say, They will come if you do not hinder them."—DA 517.

Children's Ministries Coordinator and Committee—The church elects a children's ministries coordinator to develop ministries that nurture the faith of children. The coordinator should have leadership ability as well as experience and passion for working with children.

The children's ministries coordinator works with the pastor and board to establish a children's ministries committee to provide ministries for children. The committee should consist of individuals with interest and experience in working with children. Ordinarily the members include Sabbath School division leaders, Vacation Bible School leader, Adventist Junior Youth leaders, and two to three others who have a passion for ministry to children.

If the church has a children's ministries department, Vacation Bible Schools, children's branch Sabbath Schools, Neighborhood Bible Clubs, and Story Hours, they will come under the direction of children's ministries. (See p. 87.)

Everyone involved in work with children must meet Church and legal standards and requirements, such as background checks or certification. Local church leaders should consult with the conference, which will ascertain and advise as to what background checks and certifications are available and/or required. (See Notes, #8, pp. 174, 175.)

Resources—For children's ministries resources, see Notes, #9, p. 175.

Communication

Communication ministry calls for the support of every layperson, Church employee, and Church institution. The communication department promotes the use of a sound program of public relations and all contemporary communication techniques, sustainable technologies, and media in the promulgation of the gospel. The church should elect a communication secretary and, where needed, a communication committee.

"We must take every justifiable means of bringing the light before the people. Let the press be utilized, and let every advertising agency be employed that will call attention to the work."—6T 36.

"Means will be devised to reach hearts. Some of the methods used in this work will be different from the methods used in the work in the past."—Ev 105.

Communication Secretary—The communication secretary should have the ability to meet people and rightly represent the Church, sound judgment, good organization, effective writing skills, and a willingness to carry out assignments.

The secretary gathers and disseminates news to local media, cooperates with the conference communication director, and presents periodic reports to the business meeting. The conference communication department provides appropriate instruction and help to communication secretaries.

The pastor, who is primarily responsible for the communication program of the church, will work closely in an advisory capacity with the communication secretary or committee.

Any department or organization may appoint an individual to provide the communication secretary or committee with information about newsworthy events.

Communication Committee—In a large church a communication committee may more adequately handle the many facets of the public relations and communication program. The church elects the committee, and the communication secretary serves as chairperson. Members of the committee may be assigned specific communication responsibilities, such as working with the press, media producers and online personnel, and internal church media. If there is a nearby Church institution, a member of its public relations or communication staff should be invited to sit with the committee.

Central Communication Committee—If several churches in an area arrange for a central communication committee, the communication secretary of each church should be a member and should work in harmony with any general plan that will better coordinate the handling of news and other media activities for the cooperating churches. The establishment of this committee would be initiated by the conference communication director. Meetings of the central committee would be called and presided over by a chairperson selected by the group.

Education

Church entities operate schools from kindergarten through university levels for the purpose of transmitting to students the Church's ideals, beliefs, attitudes, values, habits, and customs. The source, the means, and the aim of Adventist education are a true knowledge of God, fellowship and companionship with Him in study and service, and likeness to Him in character development.

Education Secretary—The church elects an education secretary to promote and generate support for Christian education. The secretary is a member of the Home and School Association executive committee and works in cooperation with the association.

Home and School Association—A church with a school shall establish a Home and School Association, the purpose of which is to provide parent education and unite the home, the school, and the church in endeavors to provide Christian education for the children. Parents of students, school patrons, and church members should be encouraged to be active members of the association.

Home and School Association officers shall be a leader, assistant leader, secretary-treasurer, librarian, and the educational secretary. (See p. 179.) To give continuity, some of the officers should be elected for second terms. All shall be members of the church.

The leader of the association shall be a member with success in training children, whose mind is open to new ideas, and who believes in the importance of Christian education.

The secretary-treasurer keeps the records of the association and reports to the director of the conference education department at the beginning and end of each school year. Association funds are channeled through the church/school treasurer, kept as a separate account, and audited under denominational policy.

The principal is an ex officio member of the Home and School Association committee.

Church School Board—The administrative body of every elementary (primary) school and junior academy (partial high school) operated by one church shall be a church school board elected by the church or a school committee appointed by the church board. Thus this body may be a separate school board, the church board, or a school committee of the church board appointed for this purpose. Division working policies explain the functions of school boards.

School board members should be chosen for their consecration, their belief in and loyalty to the principles of Christian education, their good judgment and tact, their experience in school matters, and their financial judgment and ability. They should believe in and be willing to follow denominational educational policies and recommendations.

If two or more churches jointly operate what is known as a multiconstituent school, the administrative body shall be drawn from the constituent churches.

One or more members of the school board should be chosen from among the members of the church board, so that the school board may be closely related to the church board.

The pastor should be a member of the school board. If the school is operated by more than one church, generally the pastors of the participating churches concerned are members of the board.

In junior academies and elementary schools, the principal or head teacher should be a member of the board.

Some members of the board may be parents of children attending the school, so the board may profit from parental viewpoints and counsel resulting from close observation and experience.

The school board officers shall be a chairperson and a secretary. If the school is operated by one church, the church elects the chairperson.

In multiconstituent school boards, additional officers shall include a treasurer, a vice chairperson, and an assistant secretary. At its first meeting after its election, a union school board elects its own chairperson from among its members. In the event that agreement between the churches is not possible, the appointment will be made by the conference board of education or the conference committee. The principal of the school generally is appointed secretary of the board.

Any action of a multiconstituent school board that involves the supporting churches in financial obligations must be submitted to their respective boards for approval.

Where a separate school board is elected, one of two plans may be followed to establish time of election and term of office: (1) all the members may be elected at the close of the calendar or fiscal year and function for one year; (2) the members of the first board may be chosen for terms of one, two, and three years, respectively, with replacement members being chosen each succeeding year for a term of three years. The purpose of this plan is to have a nucleus of experienced members on the board to ensure a continuity of policy. When a midterm vacancy is filled, the new member serves the remainder of the original term.

The school board or school committee should meet at a regular time and place at least once each month during the school year.

The school board chairperson calls meetings, presides, sees that the actions of the board are carried out, and countersigns all financial orders issued by the secretary. The chairperson is a member ex officio of the elementary school and junior academy inspection committee, which surveys and evaluates the school and its work.

The secretary keeps a permanent record of meetings, issues orders for money to pay accounts or obligations, and carries on correspondence for the board.

Where one church operates a school, the work of the treasurer is usually carried by the church treasurer or an assistant church treasurer, who receives tuition and other money, pays out money on the order of the secretary (countersigned by the chairperson), keeps a careful account of all transfers, and at each monthly meeting gives a detailed report to the board. In a multiconstituent board, a treasurer is appointed by the union board.

Family Ministries

The objective of family ministries is to strengthen marriage and the family. The family was established by divine creation with marriage at its center.

As the primary setting in which values are learned and the capacity for close relationships with God and others is developed, its health is vital to the Church's disciple-making mission.

Family ministries upholds the biblical teaching related to the family and lifts up God's ideals for family living. At the same time, it brings an understanding of the brokenness experienced by individuals and families in a fallen world. The department facilitates understanding, unity, and love at home and in the family of God. It fosters reconciliation between the generations promised in the Elijah message of Malachi 4:5, 6 and extends hope and support to those who have been hurt by abuse, family dysfunction, and broken relationships. Relational growth opportunities are provided through family life education and enrichment. Individuals, married couples, and families are helped to avail themselves of professional counseling when necessary.

Ministry to families in the local church focuses on premarital guidance for couples, marriage strengthening programs, and the education of parents. Ministry to families also gives attention to the special needs of single parents and stepfamilies and provides instruction in family-to-family evangelism.

"Our work for Christ is to begin with the family, in the home. . . . There is no missionary field more important than this. . . . By many this home field has been shamefully neglected, and it is time that divine resources and remedies were presented, that this state of evil may be corrected."— AH 35.

"God designs that the families of earth shall be a symbol of the family in heaven. Christian homes, established and conducted in accordance with God's plan, are among His most effective agencies for the formation of Christian character and for the advancement of His work."—6T 430.

"The mission of the home extends beyond its own members. . . . Far more powerful than any sermon that can be preached is the influence of a true home upon human hearts and lives."—MH 352.

Family Ministries Leader(s)—An individual or married couple (see pp. 154-156 for the Church's definition of marriage) may be elected to serve as family ministries leader(s). They should model strong and growing family relationships and exhibit a sincere interest in fostering the well-being of all families. In order to be effective, the family ministries leader(s) must have an understanding of God's redemptive plan for dealing with the brokenness in relationships that sin has brought. The leader(s) also must maintain appropriate confidentiality and know when and how to encourage individuals in critical situations to seek professional counseling.

Family Ministries Committee—The board may establish a family ministries committee chaired by the family ministries leader(s).

Resources—For family ministries resources, see Notes, #10, p. 175.

Health Ministries

The Church believes its responsibility to make Christ known to the world includes a moral obligation to preserve human dignity by promoting optimal levels of physical, mental, and spiritual health.

In addition to ministering to those who are ill, this responsibility extends to the prevention of disease through effective health education and leadership in promoting optimum health, free of tobacco, alcohol, other drugs, and unclean foods. Where possible, members shall be encouraged to follow a primarily vegetarian diet.

Health Ministries Leader—For planning and implementing an efficient program, the church elects a health ministries leader and, if needed, an associate leader. The leader should be health-oriented and interested in promoting the Church's standards in healthful living among members and in the community through church-operated health ministries programs. The leader should be able to screen programs and information that are representative of the ideals and philosophy of the Church and to integrate them into an effective spiritual and physical witness.

Health Ministries Council—Where practical, a church may appoint a health ministries council to provide leadership to both members and community in the field of healthful living and to assist in cooperative soul-saving activities through a viable program of health and temperance and spiritual emphasis. The council, in collaboration with the personal ministries council, shall lead out in developing a schedule of health ministries activities that include such programs as stop-smoking plans, cooking schools, health classes, stress-control programs, and related endeavors. If not serving as chairperson, the pastor should be an ex officio member.

Health Ministries or Temperance Society—In some areas a health ministries or temperance society may be established as a separate entity distinct from Church organizations. The conference health ministries director should be involved in establishing such an entity.

World Health Ministries Sabbath Offering—The entire World Health Ministries Sabbath Offering is sent to the conference to be distributed according to policy. Upon the church's request to the conference, up to 25 percent of the offering received in the church may revert to the church for health ministries programs.

Resources—For health ministries resources, see Notes, #11, pp. 175, 176.

Music

Selecting Music Coordinators—The church should take great care in selecting music leaders, choosing only those who are thoroughly consecrated and provide appropriate music for all church worship services and meetings. Secular music or that of a questionable nature should never be introduced into our services.

Music leaders should work closely with the pastor or elders in order that musical selections harmonize with the sermon theme. The music leader is under the direction of the pastor or elders and does not work independently. The music leader should counsel with them about the music to be rendered and the selection of singers and musicians.

Selecting Musicians—Sacred music is an important part of public worship. The church must exercise care in selecting choir members and other musicians who will rightly represent Church principles. They should be members of the church, the Sabbath School, or the Adventist Youth Ministries. Because they occupy a conspicuous place in church services, they should be examples of modesty and decorum in their appearance and dress. Choir robes are optional.

Churches may have multiple choirs. A children's choir is a means of spiritual nurture, bonding to the church family, and outreach.

Public Affairs and Religious Liberty

The public affairs and religious liberty (PARL) department promotes and maintains religious liberty, with particular emphasis upon liberty of conscience. Religious liberty includes the human right to have or adopt the religion of one's choice, to change religious belief according to conscience, to manifest one's religion individually or in community with fellow believers, in worship, observance, practice, witness, and teaching, subject to respect for the equivalent rights of others.

Religious Liberty Leader—The elected religious liberty leader cooperates with both the pastor and the conference or union PARL department. The leader should be of positive spiritual influence, able to meet the general public, interested in public affairs, proficient as a correspondent, and concerned with the preservation of liberty for God's people.

Religious Liberty Associations—Each church is considered an informal religious liberty association, and every church member is considered a member of the association. The pastor or an elder is the chairperson.

Resources—For Public Affairs and Religious Liberty resources, see Notes, #12, p. 176.

Publishing Ministries

Publishing ministries coordinates and promotes literature evangelism under supervision of the publishing ministries council and the appropriate publishing organization for the territory. It assists other departments in the promotion, sale, and distribution of subscription magazines and other missionary literature. The department works with the pastor and other departments in planning for systematic ways to involve members in publishing ministries.

"There are many places in which the voice of the minister cannot be heard, places which can be reached only by our publications—the books, papers, and tracts filled with the Bible truths that the people need."—CM 4.

The mission of publishing ministries is evangelism and the nurture of church members. Ellen G. White encouraged members to "sell or to give away our literature."—CM 91.

Selling Through Literature Evangelists—"God calls for workers from every church among us to enter His service as canvasser evangelists [literature evangelists]."—CM 20.

Giving Away (Sharing) by Church Members—"Let every believer scatter broadcast tracts and leaflets and books containing the message for this time."—CM 21.

Publishing Ministries Coordinator—The church elects a publishing ministries coordinator to provide leadership in literature evangelism activities.

Publishing Ministries Council—The board appoints the publishing ministries council, which works under the board's direction. The publishing ministries coordinator chairs the council. The pastor, personal ministries leader, and personal ministries secretary serve as ex officio members. Members should have interest and experience in literature evangelism.

Resources—For publishing ministries resources, see Notes, #13, p. 176.

Sabbath School and Personal Ministries

Sabbath School

The Sabbath School, the primary religious education program of the Church, has four purposes: study of the Scripture, fellowship, community outreach, and world mission emphasis. The General Conference Sabbath School and Personal Ministries Department distributes the Sabbath School Bible study guide for all age levels, provides designs for Sabbath School programming within the context of the various world division cultures, provides resources and training systems for Sabbath School teachers, and promotes world mission Sabbath School offerings.

"The Sabbath school is an important branch of the missionary work, not only because it gives to young and old a knowledge of God's Word, but because it awakens in them a love for its sacred truths, and a desire to study them for themselves; above all, it teaches them to regulate their lives by its holy teachings."—CSW 10, 11.

"The Sabbath school, if rightly conducted, is one of God's great instrumentalities to bring souls to a knowledge of the truth."—CSW 115.

Officers of the Sabbath School Council—The church elects Sabbath School officers and members of the Sabbath School council. Officers include the superintendent and any assistant superintendents; secretary and any assistant secretaries; a leader for each division, including adult and extension divisions; children's ministries coordinator and/or Vacation Bible School director; and Investment secretary.

The officers, teachers, and all Sabbath School members should cooperate with other departments in all outreach (missionary) work, as well as carrying on Sabbath School evangelism by means of regular Sabbath School classes and such activities as Decision Days, pastors' Bible classes, Community Guest Days, Vacation Bible Schools, and branch Sabbath Schools, including Neighborhood Bible Clubs and Story Hours.

The Sabbath School council is the administrative body of the Sabbath School. It consists of the superintendent (who serves as chairperson), any assistant superintendents, secretary (who serves as secretary), any assistant secretaries, division leaders, Investment secretary, personal ministries leader, children's ministries coordinator and/or Vacation Bible School director, an elder (appointed by the board or by the board of elders), and the pastor.

As soon as possible after the officers are elected, the superintendent should call a council meeting to appoint, as needed for the various divisions, other officers who do not serve as members of the council. These may include assistant division leaders, division secretaries, music directors, pianists and/or organists, and greeters.

In addition to the appointed officers listed above, the council studies the need of all divisions and groups and appoints teachers whose names are submitted to the board for approval. To maintain both the integrity of the Sabbath School lesson curriculum and the quality of teaching, the council should exercise great care in choosing teachers. Particularly when selecting teachers for the children's divisions, the council should consult with division leaders. All teachers shall be members of the church in regular standing.

The council is responsible for the successful operation of the entire Sabbath School through the superintendent. The council should meet regularly as needed. The council should ensure that program helps and materials, including the Sabbath School Bible study guide prepared by the General Conference, are supplied in sufficient quantities.

Sabbath School Superintendent and Other Sabbath School Officers—The superintendent is the leading officer of the Sabbath School and should begin planning for its smooth and effective operation as soon as elected. The superintendent should support the plans and emphases of the conference Sabbath School department and should implement decisions of the Sabbath School council concerning the operation of the Sabbath School. The church may elect one or more assistant superintendents.

The secretary should complete the quarterly report on the appropriate form immediately after the last Sabbath of the quarter and mail it before the deadline to the conference Sabbath School and personal ministries directors. The secretary also should place a copy in the secretary's permanent file, give copies to the superintendent and the pastor, and present it at the business meeting.

The Investment secretary promotes the Investment plan for mission support in all Sabbath School divisions and keeps all members informed as the program progresses.

The Vacation Bible School (VBS) director leads in organizing, promoting, and launching community evangelism through the annual VBS. The church may assign this responsibility to the children's ministries coordinator.

The council may appoint a music director for the Sabbath School in consultation with division leaders. As an expression of worship, music should glorify God. Singers and other musicians should be as carefully selected as are the leaders for other parts of the Sabbath School service and should be measured by the same standards. (See pp. 95, 150.) The council also may appoint pianists and organists for the divisions.

Sabbath School Division Leaders—The church board elects a leader for each division. The Sabbath School council may appoint assistant division leaders as needed. The Sabbath School Handbook, available from the Adventist Book Center or the conference Sabbath School department, contains information about all divisions, from beginners through adult and the extension division, which cares for those unable to attend Sabbath School.

Sabbath School Teachers—The Sabbath School council chooses and the church board approves Sabbath School teachers. They should have an aptitude for teaching and be willing to study ways to improve their teaching abilities. They should be diligent in preparation, regular and punctual in attendance, and examples in the daily study of the Sabbath School Bible study guide.

The council should make special effort to select teachers for children and youth who have an interest in those age levels and ability to meet their needs. Everyone involved in work with the children's divisions must meet Church and legal standards and requirements, such as background checks or certification. Local church leaders should consult with the conference, which will ascertain and advise as to what background checks and certifications are available and/or required. (See Notes, #8, pp. 174, 175.) All teachers should be encouraged to participate in the teacher training courses available through the conference Sabbath School department.

Every Sabbath School should have a weekly teachers' meeting.

Realizing that "none but those who have fortified the mind with the truths of the Bible will stand through the last great conflict" (GC 593, 594), Sabbath School leaders should strongly encourage regular systematic study of the Word. The Sabbath School Bible study guide is designed to encourage daily feasting on the Word, a practice that has done much to maintain unity throughout the Church. Every member should have access to the appropriate age-level Sabbath School Bible study guide published by the General Conference and/or division. Similarly, every leader and teacher should have access to the helps produced for the various Sabbath School divisions by the General Conference and/or division.

Teachers should have at least 30 minutes during which to teach their classes.

Sabbath School Offerings—The Sabbath School secretary should accurately record Sabbath School offerings and pass them on to the treasurer as soon as possible. Extension division offerings should be added to the regular Sabbath School offerings. Many Sabbath Schools take offerings for Sabbath School expense. With the exception of that expense fund, all Sabbath School offerings are for the support of the mission fields and are to be passed on in their entirety by the treasurer to the conference. These funds include the regular weekly Sabbath School offering, the Thirteenth Sabbath Offering, Sabbath School Investment, and Birthday-Thank Offering. Each is to be identified as a separate fund in the financial system of the church. Mission funds are distributed according to policy. No mission funds may be retained by the church or conference.

The Sabbath School expense offering and the mission offering, where the calendar of offerings is being used, shall not be taken as one offering and divided according to an agreed-upon formula or percentage. The offerings may be taken as combined offering where the church is operating under a division-approved combined offering plan.

Resources—For Sabbath School and personal ministries resources, see Notes, #14, p. 176.

Personal Ministries

Personal ministries provides resources and trains members to unite their efforts with those of the pastor and officers in soul-winning service. It also has primary responsibility for programs assisting those in need.

Personal Ministries Council—The personal ministries council guides the outreach (missionary) efforts of the church and works under the direction of the board. The council should meet at least once each month and should consist of the pastor, an elder, the treasurer, and leaders of the other departments and auxiliary services functioning in that congregation. The personal ministries council may assign subcommittees for specialized tasks. All subcommittees report to the personal ministries council. The personal ministries council and leader are responsible for organizing small group ministries.

Personal Ministries Officers—The church elects the personal ministries officers, including the leader, assistants (as needed), and the secretary.

The leader trains and directs members in outreach (missionary) service and chairs the personal ministries council. The leader reports in the monthly church outreach (missionary) Sabbath service and business meetings about total outreach (missionary) activities of the congregation. Assistants may be assigned to coordinate the Bible correspondence school, Bible evangelism, literature distribution, Ingathering (or equivalent appeals), small group ministries, member training, and other soul-winning programs.

The secretary serves as representative of the Adventist Book Center for all departments of the church and works with the leader in developing the outreach (missionary) programs of the church.

Adventist Men—Adventist Men is a subsidiary of the personal ministries department. It includes lay preaching efforts, prison ministry, and Community Services.

Bible School Coordinator—The Bible school coordinator organizes and coordinates the church's Bible school outreach ministry to the community. The coordinator should work closely with the pastor, the interest coordinator, and the personal ministries leader.

Adventist Community Services Leader or Dorcas Society Leader—The church elects the Adventist Community Services leader or Dorcas Society leader, assistant leaders (as needed), and secretary-treasurer of Adventist Community Services, which in some areas is known as the Dorcas Society. (See Notes, #15, p. 177.) This organization gathers and prepares clothing, food and other supplies for those in need and works closely with the Adventist Men, deacons, deaconesses, and other church departments in community outreach. Adventist Community Services or Dorcas Society ministry, however, includes more than giving material aid. It focuses on identifying needs and responding with services based on these specific needs. Examples are educational seminars, community development, visiting, counseling, and other services relevant to the community.

The Adventist Community Services Leader or Dorcas Society Leader is a member of the Personal Ministries Council and the church board. If the church operates a Community Services center, the personal ministries council is its governing committee. The Council appoints the director of the center, who is a member of the Council as well as the church board.

Ministry to People With Disabilities—This ministry functions under the personal ministries council and develops programs for members and others with disabilities. It should create witnessing programs, recommend how to make church facilities more accessible, help solve transportation problems, and recommend ways to involve members with disabilities. The coordinator of Ministry to People With Disabilities serves as a liaison with organizations providing services for people with disabilities, such as Christian Record Services, and promotes Christian Record Services programs.

Resources—For Sabbath School and personal ministries resources, see Notes, #14, p. 176.

Stewardship Ministries

Stewardship ministries encourages members to respond to God's grace by dedicating all they have to Him. Stewardship responsibility involves more than just money. It includes, but is not limited to, the proper care and use of the body, mind, time, abilities, spiritual gifts, relationships, influence, language, the environment, and material possessions. The department assists members in their partnership with God in completing His mission through the proper utilization of all of His gifts and resources.

When the Spirit of God takes possession of the life, "those whose hearts are filled with the love of Christ will follow the example of Him who for our sake became poor, that through His poverty we might be made rich. Money, time, influence—all the gifts they have received from God's hand, they will value only as a means of advancing the work of the gospel."—AA 71.

Stewardship Ministries Leader—The stewardship ministries leader should practice the principles of Christian stewardship and should have an understanding of the spiritual and financial ministry of the Church. The leader will work in cooperation with the conference stewardship ministries director, the pastor, and the board. The leader acts as a liaison between the conference stewardship ministries department and the congregation.

Resources—For stewardship ministries resources, see Notes, #16, p. 177.

Women's Ministries

Women's ministries upholds, encourages, and challenges women in their daily walk as disciples of Jesus Christ and as members of His church.

Its objectives are to foster spiritual growth and renewal; affirm that women are of immeasurable worth by virtue of their creation and redemption, equip them for service, and offer women's perspectives on church issues; minister to the broad spectrum of women's needs, with regard for multicultural and multiethnic perspectives; cooperate with other departments to facilitate ministry to women and of women; build good will among women to encourage mutual support and creative exchange of ideas; mentor and encourage women and create paths for their involvement in the church; and find ways and means to challenge each woman to use her gifts to further global mission.

Women's Ministries Leader and Committee—The elected women's ministries leader develops specific ministries to nurture women and equip them for service. She serves as chairperson of the women's ministries committee and encourages ideas and plans that maximize women's contributions to the mission of the Church.

The leader assists the board with integrating activities and programs for women into the larger church program. She keeps the church informed of the contribution of women's ministries to church life. The leader's liaison for training and resource material is the conference women's ministries director.

The women's ministries leader should be a sensitive, caring woman with a burden for women's ministry and concerns, a balance in her perspectives, an ability to encourage other women to cultivate their spiritual gifts, and an ability to work well with women in the church, the pastor, and the board.

The women's ministries committee fosters ministry to women in the church. This committee should be composed of those interested in the broad spectrum of women's needs and services and those with varied talents and experience.

Resources—For women's ministries resources, see Notes, #17, p. 177.

Youth Ministries

The various youth organizations of the church should work closely with the youth ministries department of the conference.

Adventist Youth Ministries (AYM)—The church works for and with its youth through the AYM. Under the AYM, youth are to work together, in cooperation with the wider church community, towards the development of a strong youth ministry that includes spiritual, mental, and physical development of each individual, Christian social interaction, and an active witnessing program that supports the general soul-winning plans of the church. The goal of AYM should be to involve all youth in activities that will lead them to active church membership and train them for Christian service.

AYM Mission—To lead young people into a saving relationship with Jesus Christ and help them embrace His call to discipleship.

AYM Motto—The love of Christ compels us.

AYM Aim—The Advent Message to all the world in my generation.

The youth ministries program of the church comprises three broad categories, namely: Junior Youth (Adventurers: ages 6-9 and Pathfinders: ages 10-15), Senior Youth (Ambassadors: ages 16-21 and Young Adults: ages 22-30+), and Public Campus Students: ages 16-30+.

God said to Moses, "And these words which I command you today shall be in your heart. You shall teach them diligently to your children, and shall talk of them when you sit in your house, when you walk by the way, when you lie down, and when you rise up. You shall bind them as a sign on your hand, and they shall be as frontlets between your eyes. You shall write them on the doorposts of your house and on your gates" (Deut. 6:6-9).

The apostle Paul added, "Let no one despise your youth, but be an example to the believers in word, in conduct, in love, in spirit, in faith, in purity" (1 Tim. 4:12).

"We have an army of youth today who can do much if they are properly directed and encouraged. . . . We want them to be blessed of God. We want them to act a part in well-organized plans for helping other youth."— GCB, Jan. 29, 30, 1893, p. 24.

"When the youth give their hearts to God, our responsibility for them does not cease. They must be interested in the Lord's work, and led to see that He expects them to do something to advance His cause. It is not enough to show how much needs to be done, and to urge the youth to act a part. They must be taught how to labor for the Master. They must be trained, disciplined, drilled, in the best methods of winning souls to Christ. Teach them to try in a quiet, unpretending way to help their young companions. Let different branches of missionary effort be systematically laid out, in which they may take part, and let them be given instruction and help. Thus they will learn to work for God."—GW 210.

"With such an army of workers as our youth, rightly trained, might furnish, how soon the message of a crucified, risen, and soon-coming Savior might be carried to the whole world!"—MYP 196.

While there is to be an active Adventist Youth Ministries (AYM) in every church, it is important that the youth program not be isolated from the rest of the church. In addition to their AYM participation, youth should be integrated into responsible leadership and in all lines of church work. As young elders, deacons, and deaconesses, for example, they can work with and learn from experienced officers.

"In order that the work may go forward in all its branches, God calls for youthful vigor, zeal, and courage. He has chosen the youth to aid in the advancement of His cause. To plan with clear mind and execute with courageous hand demands fresh, uncrippled energies. Young men and women are invited to give God the strength of their youth, that through the exercise of their powers, through keen thought and vigorous action, they may bring glory to Him and salvation to their fellow men."—GW 67.

Adventist Youth Ministries Committee—The Adventist Youth Ministries (AYM) Committee is the umbrella organization in the church for the general planning of the youth ministry program. (See pp. 133, 134.) The AYM Committee includes the following church-elected officers: Young Adults leader, Public Campus Ministries leader/coordinator, Ambassador leader, Pathfinder director, Adventurer director, plus the personal ministries leader, youth Sabbath School division leader, children's ministries leader, health ministries leader, principal of the school, the AYM sponsor, and the pastor.

If there are no distinct Ambassador ministry or young adults ministries established in the church, or until such time as they are established, the AYM Committee will plan for the senior youth ministry to include both age groups.

In parts of the world where there is no Pathfinder or Adventurer ministry, or until such time as they are organized, the AYM Committee will plan for appropriate activities for the junior youth.

The AYM leader (formerly known as the AYS director), who is a member of the board, chairs this committee. The committee should meet as necessary to develop short- and long-range goals and plans for a successful ministry. (See Notes, #18, pp. 177, 178.)

Young Adults Ministries Committee—The Young Adults Ministries Committee is responsible for Young Adult activities and works in coordination with the Adventist Youth Ministries (AYM) Committee.

The church elects the following Young Adults Ministries officers: leader, associate leader, secretary-treasurer, and music director. This group forms the nucleus for the Young Adults Ministries Committee, which appoints other officers for the respective activities.

Public Campus Ministries—Strengthening the Youth Ministries of the church, Public Campus Ministries (PCM), in collaboration with the Adventist Ministry to College and University Students (AMiCUS), provides vision and strategic planning for ministry to and support for Seventh-day Adventist students (ages 16-30+) who attend college or university institutions not operated by the Seventh-day Adventist Church.

Public Campus Ministries Leader/Coordinator—The church may appoint a Public Campus Ministries leader/coordinator to develop an intentional ministry with the purpose of caring for the special needs of college or university students in institutions not operated by the Seventh-day Adventist Church, in consultation with and support of the Adventist Youth Ministries Committee.

Ambassador Ministry—The Ambassador Ministry provides a specialized program to meet the needs of youth, ages 16 to 21. It offers young people in this age group organization and structure, and promotes their active involvement in the church, locally and globally. The ministry is designed to strengthen the current senior youth ministry of the Church. It challenges them to experience and share a personal relationship with Christ, helps them develop a lifestyle that is consistent with the Seventh-day Adventist belief system, provides training in diverse vocational interests, and provides them with a safe environment for the wholesome development of lifelong friendships. Its activities are to be carried out in accordance with conference policies and in coordination with the AYM Committee of the local church.

Ambassador Committee—The Ambassador Committee is responsible for Ambassador activities and works in coordination with the Adventist Youth Ministries (AYM) Committee.

The church elects the following Ambassador officers: leader, associate leader, secretary-treasurer, assistant secretary-treasurer, and music director. This group forms the Ambassador Committee which appoints other officers for the respective activities.

Pathfinder Club—The Pathfinder Club provides a church-centered outlet for the spirit of adventure and exploration, in the context of spiritual development and soul-winning, for ages 10 to 15. Activities are carefully tailored to include outdoor living, nature exploration, crafts, hobbies, or vocations.

Pathfinder Committee—The Pathfinder Club director and deputy directors are elected by the church. (See pp. 105, 179.) If two deputy directors are elected, there should be one male and one female. One of the deputy directors may also serve as club secretary and treasurer. The director is a member of the board and the Adventist Youth Ministries (AYM) Committee.

Additional Pathfinder staff may include instructors of craft and nature classes and counselors who are each responsible for a unit of six to eight Pathfinders.

Resource materials are available from the conference youth ministries director.

Everyone involved in work with minor children must meet Church and legal standards and requirements, such as background checks or certification. Local church leaders should consult with the conference, which will ascertain and advise as to what background checks and certifications are available and/or required. (See Notes, #7, pp. 168, 169.)

Adventurer Club—The Adventurer Club provides home and church programs for parents with 6-to-9-year-old children. It is designed to stimulate the children's curiosity and includes age-specific activities that involve both parents and child in recreational activities, simple crafts, appreciation of God's creation, and other activities that are of interest to that age. All is carried out with a spiritual focus, setting the stage for participation in the church as a Pathfinder.

Adventurer Committee—The church elects the club director and associates. (See pp. 104, 178.) Additional staff members are selected by the administrative staff of the club. The director is a member of the Adventist Youth Ministries (AYM) Committee.

Resource materials are available from the conference youth ministries director.

Everyone involved in work with minor children must meet Church and legal standards and requirements, such as background checks or certification. Local church leaders should consult with the conference, which will ascertain and advise as to what background checks and certifications are available and/or required. (See Notes, #8, pp. 174, 175.)

AYM Officers—The leaders/directors of the four youth ministry entities must exemplify Christlike graces and have a burden for soul winning and contagious enthusiasm. In helping motivate youth to work together and take responsibilities, the leaders/directors will be in the background— guiding, counseling, and encouraging youth, helping them gain experience and the joys of achievement. The leaders/directors should study the youth profile of the church and seek to involve every eligible youth in the Adventist Youth Ministries (AYM).

The leaders/directors will keep in touch with the pastor, their respective sponsors, and the conference youth ministries director, taking advantage of opportunities for in-service training and leading their respective ministry into a cooperative relationship with the church and the conference.

The associate leaders/deputy directors (if needed) will assist the leaders/directors and perform leadership duties when the leaders/directors are absent. The respective committees may assign additional responsibilities to the associate leaders/directors.

The secretary-treasurers will keep a record of the activities of their respective ministries, submit monthly reports on forms provided to the conference youth ministries director, and encourage youth to report their witnessing activities during the ten-minute personal ministries period.

The respective assistant secretary-treasurers (if needed) assist with the secretary- treasurers' work as assigned.

AYM Sponsor—The Adventist Youth Ministries (AYM) sponsor may be an elder or other person on the board who understands the objectives of the AYM, is sympathetic with youth and their involvement in the church's ministries, and will serve as a valued counselor to the youth. The sponsor serves as a guide or counselor to AYM officers and joins them regularly in AYM Committee meetings. The sponsor will work with the AYM leader to present the ministry's needs to the board.

The sponsor should become acquainted with the conference youth ministries director and keep the director informed of changes in officer personnel and other AYM matters. Along with AYM leaders, the sponsor should attend conference youth training institutes to keep informed about developments in youth ministry.

For the sake of continuity, the sponsor, if possible, should serve multiple terms.

Everyone involved in work with minor children must meet Church and legal standards and requirements, such as background checks or certification. Local church leaders should consult with the conference, which will ascertain and advise as to what background checks and certifications are available and/or required. (See Notes, #7, pp. 168, 169.)

Resources—For youth ministries resources, see Notes, #17, p. 171.

Induction Service

All newly elected officers of the local church may be included in an induction service conducted by a pastor holding a current license or credential. If no pastor is available, an elder of the church may conduct the service for officers other than elders, deacons, and deaconesses. If the church holds an induction service for newly elected officers, it should include leaders of all departments and other organizations.

CHAPTER 9

Elections

The election of church officers who will perform their duties prayerfully, seriously, and competently is an important work. This chapter outlines the election procedure, from appointment of the nominating committee to filling vacancies between annual elections.

Nominating Committee and the Election Process

Officers are elected every one or two years (see p. 72) through an appointed nominating committee. This committee brings its report to the church, which then votes on the names presented. This procedure enables the church to give careful study to each name prior to election and avoids the competitive element that may arise when nominations are made from the floor.

The nominating committee shall study the needs of the church and inquire into the fitness of members to serve in the different offices. This is another reason officers shall not be nominated from the floor or by general ballot.

The size of the nominating committee will range from five members in a small church to a larger number in a large church. The number to be chosen is left to the discretion of each church and should be studied by the board. A suitable recommendation then will be brought to the church, using a minimum of time in the Sabbath worship hour.

When and How the Nominating Committee Is Appointed—The nominating committee should be appointed early in the closing quarter of the church year and should report at least three weeks before the final Sabbath of the church year.

The pastor or district leader or, in the absence of the pastor or district leader, the elder should bring the matter to the attention of the church. The church shall then appoint an organizing committee responsible to nominate the nominating committee. This organizing committee may be chosen in one of two ways:

1. By nominations, verbal or written, from the floor. If verbal nominations are made, no member may nominate more than one person. The effort of one individual or a small group to dictate to the entire membership is disapproved. Every effort should be made to ensure fair representation in the composition of the organizing committee. Everything

of a political nature should be avoided. The pastor or district leader shall serve as chairperson of this organizing committee. If a pastor or district leader has not yet been appointed to serve as church leader, the chairperson of this organizing committee shall be appointed by the board from among the members of the organizing committee. The size of the organizing committee should be five to seven more than the number of board members.

2.   By the church authorizing the board, together with five to seven additional persons chosen by the church (see preceding paragraph), to function as the organizing committee. If this method is adopted, the chairperson of the board normally serves as chairperson of the organizing committee (see p. 32).

How the Process Works—The steps of the nominating process are:

1.   The church appoints by vote an organizing committee by one of the two methods listed above.

2.   The organizing committee recommends names to the church for the nominating committee, with a recommendation for secretary. Every effort should be made to ensure fair representation in the composition of the nominating committee.

3.   By vote, the church appoints the nominating committee and the secretary.

4.   The pastor or district leader is an ex officio member and serves as chairperson of the nominating committee. Should the pastor or district leader choose not to serve as chairperson, or if a pastor or district leader has not been appointed to the church, the organizing committee shall recommend the name from the proposed nominating committee to serve as chairperson.

5.   The nominating committee meets to prepare the list of officers that it will present to the church for approval.

6.   By vote, the church appoints its officers for the ensuing year.

Who Should Be Members of the Nominating Committee—Only members in regular standing should be chosen to serve on the nominating committee. They should be persons of good judgment who have the welfare and prosperity of the church at heart.

Work of the Nominating Committee—The chairperson should call a meeting of the committee as soon as possible after its election. With earnest prayer the committee should begin preparing a list of nominees for all offices. Nominees must be members in regular standing of the church making the appointments. The list of nominees will be presented to the church at a Sabbath service or at a specially called business meeting. In making their selections, the committee may counsel with others who are well informed. This committee does not nominate either the pastor or the assistant pastor(s), who are appointed by the conference.

The list of officers to be considered by the nominating committee may vary with size of membership. A larger church may determine it needs more officers. A smaller church may have fewer. The committee deals with all leadership positions except Sabbath School teachers, who are recommended by the Sabbath School council and approved by the board. See Notes, #1, pp. 178, 179, for a list of possible officers.

Nominating Committee to Get Consent of Prospective Officers—Having nominated persons who are faithful, loyal members of the local church, except when the conference has approved an exception (see p. 74, "Work of Elders Is Local"), the appropriate members of the committee should inform them of their nominations and secure their consent to serve.

Members May Appear Before the Nominating Committee—Members desiring to appear before the committee to make suggestions or objections should be given opportunity to do so. After they have addressed the committee and retired from the room, the committee should consider their comments and then make its report to the church.

Nominating Committee Discussions Are Confidential—All inquiries and discussions of the committee are confidential. It is a violation of Christian ethics and the spirit of the golden rule for a member of the committee to repeat outside of the committee any personal or sensitive information discussed. To offend in this regard is reason for excluding the committee member from future participation in the work of a nominating committee. Should the necessity arise for inquiries to be made outside the committee, the chairperson should make them.

Reporting to the Church—The nominating committee's report is presented to the church as a whole and not to the church board, which has no jurisdiction in the process. The report may be presented at a Sabbath service or at a specially called business meeting.

When the nominating committee is ready to report, the chairperson should make appropriate remarks to the church. A copy of the report should be placed in the hands of members or read aloud by the secretary of the committee. The chairperson should announce that the church will vote on the report one or two weeks later.

Every member should vote in the election of officers. Election is by majority vote of those present and voting.

Objections to the Report of the Nominating Committee— Members may object to the nominating committee's report and should present their objections in person to the committee before the second reading of the report by making an appointment through the chairperson or pastor. Or, at the time of the second reading of the report, a member may request that the whole report be referred without discussion to the committee for further consideration. It is the usual procedure for the chairperson to accept the referral. However, if the request becomes a motion, it is nondebatable and is decided by majority vote.

The chairperson should announce when and where the committee will meet to hear objections. At that time members making objections, or any other member who desires to do so, should appear before the committee. If the election is deferred because of objections, it would be a serious matter for those raising objections to fail to appear before the committee.

After giving due consideration to the objections presented, the committee will exercise its judgment as to whether or not any change is warranted in the committee's recommendation to the church business meeting. When the report is again presented, the church proceeds to vote on the report of the committee.

Trivial or groundless objections to any name should never be made, but if there are serious reasons that any nomination should be changed, these reasons should be stated to the nominating committee.

Filling Vacancies Between Elections—If an office of the church becomes vacant during the term of office because of death, removal, resignation, or any other reason, the board nominates a successor to fill the vacancy for the remainder of the term of office and submits the nomination to the church for election.

Delegates to Local Conference Session

Administrative authority in a conference originates with its constituency. The churches of a conference elect delegates to the conference session to represent them in the councils of the conference. The conference session elects conference personnel, grants credentials and licenses (unless the conference constitution gives its executive committee this responsibility), amends its constitution and bylaws if necessary, and transacts other business. One of its most important acts is the election of the executive committee, which functions for the constituency between sessions. In this committee is vested the delegated power and authority of all the churches of the conference.

Choosing Delegates—It is God's plan that members chosen to be delegates be trustworthy, tried, and proved, "able to reason from cause to effect," because they are to "lay the plans that shall be followed in the advancement of the work."—9T 262.

The number of delegates from each church to a conference session is determined by the conference constitution. When the time comes to select delegates, the pastor, or the head elder in cooperation with the pastor, brings the matter before the church. A committee may be appointed to nominate delegates, or the board may be asked to nominate them. Nothing of a political nature should be allowed to come into this work. Men and women of known piety and loyalty and who are able to attend the session should be nominated as delegates. (See p. 82.)

When the committee or board has completed its work, it reports its nominees to the church. The church then votes on the nominations. No church officer is a delegate ex officio. After the election, the clerk fills out the delegates' credential blanks and returns them to the secretary of the conference. The delegates become the representatives of the church, to unite with the delegates of other churches to transact all business coming before the conference session.

Delegates to a union conference/mission session are chosen by the conference, not by the churches. The delegates to a General Conference Session are chosen by the divisions and the union conferences/missions.

Duty of Delegates—Delegates to a conference session are not chosen to represent merely the church or conference. They should view the work as a whole, remembering their responsibility for the welfare of the worldwide work of the Church. It is not permissible for church or conference delegations to organize or attempt to direct their votes as a unit. Nor is it permissible for the delegates from a large church or the conference to claim preeminence in directing affairs in a conference session. Each delegate should be susceptible to the direction of the Holy Spirit and vote according to personal convictions. Any church or conference officer or leader attempting to control the votes of a group of delegates would be considered disqualified for holding office.

Responsibility of Conference Officers—The local church has no authority outside its own body. It unites with other churches in the conference in delegating authority and responsibility to the conference officers and executive committee to carry on the work of the conference between sessions. Conference officers are answerable to the conference as a whole and not to any one church.

Conference Executive Committee—Conference executive committee members are elected to represent the work in the entire conference, not that of one church, district, or institution. Each member should foster all interests of the work in all parts of the field and make decisions only after prayerful and careful study. Decisions of the committee are not to be controlled or influenced by any church, group, or individual.

CHAPTER 10

Services and Other Meetings

General Principles

The apostle John declared that "true worshipers will worship the Father in spirit and truth; for the Father is seeking such to worship Him" (John 4:23).

"Although God dwells not in temples made with hands, yet He honors with His presence the assemblies of His people. He has promised that when they come together to seek Him, to acknowledge their sins, and to pray for one another, He will meet with them by His Spirit. But those who assemble to worship Him should put away every evil thing. Unless they worship Him in spirit and truth and in the beauty of holiness, their coming together will be of no avail."—PK 50.

Purpose of Services and Meetings—The purpose of all services and meetings is to worship God for His creative work and for the benefits of His salvation; to understand His Word, His teachings, and His purposes; to fellowship in faith and love; to witness about our personal faith in Christ's atoning sacrifice at the cross; and to learn how to fulfill the gospel commission of making disciples in all the world (Matt. 28:19, 20).

Reverence for the House of Worship—"To the humble, believing soul, the house of God on earth is the gate of heaven. The song of praise, the prayer, the words spoken by Christ's representatives, are God's appointed agencies to prepare a people for the church above, for that loftier worship into which there can enter nothing that defileth.

"From the sacredness which was attached to the earthly sanctuary, Christians may learn how they should regard the place where the Lord meets with His people. . . . God Himself gave the order of His service, exalting it high above everything of a temporal nature.

"The house is the sanctuary for the family, and the closet or the grove the most retired place for individual worship; but the church is the sanctuary for the congregation. There should be rules in regard to the time, the place, and the manner of worshiping. Nothing that is sacred, nothing that pertains to the worship of God, should be treated with carelessness or indifference."—5T 491.

Teach Children Reverence—"Parents, elevate the standard of Christianity in the minds of your children; help them to weave Jesus into their experience; teach them to have the highest reverence for the house of God and to understand that when they enter the Lord's house it should be with hearts that are softened and subdued by such thoughts as these: 'God is here; this is His house. I must have pure thoughts and the holiest motives. I must have no pride, envy, jealousy, evil surmising, hatred, or deception in my heart, for I am coming into the presence of the holy God. This is the place where God meets with and blesses His people. The high and holy One who inhabiteth eternity looks upon me, searches my heart, and reads the most secret thoughts and acts of my life.' "—5T 494.

Decorum and Quietness in the Place of Worship—"When the worshipers enter the place of meeting, they should do so with decorum, passing quietly to their seats. . . . Common talking, whispering, and laughing should not be permitted in the house of worship, either before or after the service. Ardent, active piety should characterize the worshipers.

"If some have to wait a few minutes before the meeting begins, let them maintain a true spirit of devotion by silent meditation, keeping the heart uplifted to God in prayer that the service may be of special benefit to their own hearts and lead to the conviction and conversion of other souls. They should remember that heavenly messengers are in the house. . . . If when the people come into the house of worship, they have genuine reverence for the Lord and bear in mind that they are in His presence, there will be a sweet eloquence in silence. The whispering and laughing and talking which might be without sin in a common business place should find no sanction in the house where God is worshiped. The mind should be prepared to hear the Word of God, that it may have due weight and suitably impress the heart."—5T 492.

Hospitality—"Do not forget to entertain strangers, for by so doing some have unwittingly entertained angels" (Heb. 13:2). Every church should cultivate a spirit of hospitality, an essential element of Christian life and experience. Nothing is so deadening to the spiritual life of a church as a cold, formal atmosphere that drives out hospitality and Christian fellowship. Especially selected greeters should cordially welcome visitors, who also may be welcomed at the time of the worship service.

Place of Music in Worship

Power of Music—"Music can be a great power for good, yet we do not make the most of this branch of worship. The singing is generally done from impulse or to meet special cases, and at other times those who sing are left to blunder along, and the music loses its proper effect upon the minds of those present. Music should have beauty, pathos, and power. Let the voices be lifted in songs of praise and devotion. Call to your aid, if practicable, instrumental music, and let the glorious harmony ascend to God, an acceptable offering."—4T 71.

Sing With Spirit and Understanding—"In their efforts to reach the people, the Lord's messengers are not to follow the ways of the world. In the meetings that are held, they are not to depend on worldly singers and theatrical display to awaken an interest. How can those who have no interest in the Word of God, who have never read His Word with a sincere desire to understand its truths, be expected to sing with the spirit and the understanding? . . . How can the heavenly choir join in music that is only a form? . . . "The singing is not always to be done by a few. As often as possible, let the entire congregation join."—9T 143, 144.

Pulpit Not a Forum

The Church confers no right to any pastor, elder, or other person to make the pulpit a forum for advocating disputed points of doctrine or church procedure.

Testing New Light—Members who think they have new light contrary to the established views of the Church should seek counsel from responsible leaders.

"There are a thousand temptations in disguise prepared for those who have the light of truth; and the only safety for any of us is in receiving no new doctrine, no new interpretation of the Scriptures, without first submitting it to brethren of experience. Lay it before them in a humble, teachable spirit, with earnest prayer; and if they see no light in it, yield to their judgment; for 'in the multitude of counselors there is safety.' "— 5T 293. (See also Acts 15:1-32.)

This plan was followed in the early church. When a difference of opinion arose at Antioch over an important question, the believers sent representatives to Jerusalem to submit the question to the apostles and elders. The believers in Antioch joyfully accepted the decision of the Jerusalem Council, thus preserving unity and brotherly love.

The counsel to test new light must not be regarded as deterring anyone from diligently studying the Scriptures, but rather as a protection against the infiltration of false theories and erroneous doctrines into the Church. God wants His children faithfully to search His Word for light and truth, but He does not want them to be led astray by false teachings.

"We have seen only the glimmering of divine glory and of the infinitude of knowledge and wisdom; we have, as it were, been working on the surface of the mine, when rich golden ore is beneath the surface, to reward the one who will dig for it. The shaft must be sunk deeper and yet deeper in the mine, and the result will be glorious treasure. Through a correct faith, divine knowledge will become human knowledge."— COL 113.

"New light will ever be revealed on the Word of God to him who is in living connection with the Sun of Righteousness. Let no one come to the conclusion that there is no more truth to be revealed. The diligent, prayerful seeker for truth will find precious rays of light yet to shine forth from the Word of God. Many gems are yet scattered that are to be gathered together to become the property of the remnant people of God."—CSW 34.

When new light shines forth from the sacred page to reward the earnest seeker after truth, it does not make void the old. Instead it merges with the old, causing it to grow brighter with added luster. Therefore, "the path of the just is like the shining sun, that shines ever brighter unto the perfect day" (Prov. 4:18).

Although the child of God must stand ready to accept advancing light, one must never give heed to any voice, however pious and plausible, that would lead away from the fundamental doctrines of the Bible.

"We are not to receive the words of those who come with a message that contradicts the special points of our faith. They gather together a mass of Scripture, and pile it as proof around their asserted theories. This has been done over and over again during the past fifty years. And while the Scriptures are God's Word, and are to be respected, the application of them, if such application moves one pillar from the foundation that God has sustained these fifty years, is a great mistake. He who makes such an application knows not the wonderful demonstration of the Holy Spirit that gave power and force to the past messages that have come to the people of God."—CW 32.

Importance of Maintaining Unity

It is important that we maintain "the unity of the faith" (Eph. 4:13), and just as important that we seek to "keep the unity of the Spirit in the bond of peace" (verse 3). Such unity requires caution and counsel with church leadership.

"God is leading a people out from the world upon the exalted platform of eternal truth, the commandments of God and the faith of Jesus. He will discipline and fit up His people. They will not be at variance, one believing one thing and another having faith and views entirely opposite, each moving independently of the body. Through the diversity of the gifts and governments that He has placed in the church, they will all come to the unity of the faith. If one man takes his views of Bible truth without regard to the opinion of his brethren, and justifies his course, alleging that he has a right to his own peculiar views, and then presses them upon others, how can he be fulfilling the prayer of Christ? . . .

"Though we have an individual work and an individual responsibility before God, we are not to follow our own independent judgment, regardless of the opinions and feelings of our brethren; for this course would lead to disorder in the church. It is the duty of ministers to respect the judgment of their brethren; but their relations to one another, as well as the doctrines they teach, should be brought to the test of the law and the testimony; then, if hearts are teachable, there will be no divisions among us. Some are inclined to be disorderly, and are drifting away from the great landmarks of the faith; but God is moving upon His ministers to be one in doctrine and in spirit."—TM 29, 30.

In view of these considerations, it is evident that the pulpit must be reserved for the preaching of the truths of the Divine Word and the presentation of denominational plans and policies for the advancement of the work of God, not personal views and opinions. (See pp. 34, 118, 119.)

Unauthorized Speakers—Under no circumstances should a pastor, elder, or other officer invite strangers or any unauthorized persons to conduct services. Individuals who have been removed from the ministry or who have been removed from membership in other places, or designing persons who have no authority from the church, should not be given access to the pulpit. Those worthy of confidence will be able to identify themselves by producing proper credentials.

At times it is acceptable for government officials or civic leaders to address a congregation, but all others should be excluded from the pulpit unless permission is granted by the conference. Every pastor, elder, and conference president must enforce this rule. (See pp. 34, 118, 119.)

Sabbath School and Worship Services

Sabbath School—The Sabbath School, one of our most important services, is the church at study. Every Sabbath our members and thousands of interested friends meet in Sabbath School to study God's Word systematically. All members of the church should be encouraged to attend Sabbath School and bring visitors.

Each Sabbath School should endeavor to provide appropriate age-level programs. Materials and resources are available from the conference, union, and division.

Sabbath School should promote local and worldwide mission activities, the mission offering, and significant time for Bible study. (See Notes, #1, p. 179.)

Announcements and Departmental Promotions—Thoughtful consideration should be given to the length and character of the announcements and departmental promotions during Sabbath services. If they deal with matters not specifically related to Sabbath worship or the work of the church, pastors and officers should exclude them, maintaining even in this respect a proper spirit of worship and Sabbath observance.

Many churches issue printed bulletins giving the order of service and also the announcements for the week. Where this is done, there is little or no need for oral announcements. Where no such printed provision is made, many churches make the announcements before the worship service begins. (See Notes, #2, pp. 179, 180.)

Proper consideration also should be given for the various departments to promote their programs, but great care should be exercised to safeguard the time needed for studying and preaching the Word of God.

Worship Service—The Sabbath worship service is the most important church meeting. Here members gather weekly to unite in worshipping God in a spirit of praise and thanksgiving, to hear the Word of God, to gather strength and grace to fight the battles of life, and to learn God's will for them in soul-winning service. Reverence, simplicity, and promptness should characterize the service.

Skill, Study, and Planning Required—"Is it not your duty to put some skill and study and planning into the matter of conducting religious meetings—how they shall be conducted so as to do the greatest amount of good, and leave the very best impression upon all who attend?"—RH, Apr. 14, 1885.

"Our God is a tender, merciful Father. His service should not be looked upon as a heart-saddening, distressing exercise. It should be a pleasure to worship the Lord and to take part in His work. . . . Christ and Him crucified should be the theme of contemplation, of conversation, and of our most joyful emotion. . . . As we express our gratitude we are approximating to the worship of the heavenly hosts. 'Whoso offereth praise glorifieth'· God. Psalm 50:23. Let us with reverent joy come before our Creator, with 'thanksgiving, and the voice of melody.' Isaiah 51:3."—SC 103, 104.

Form of Service—The Sabbath morning service has two main divisions: the congregational response in praise and adoration, expressed in song, prayer, and gifts, and the message from the Word of God. (See Notes, #3, pp. 180, 181.)

There is no set form or order for public worship. A short order of service is usually better suited to the real spirit of worship. Long preliminaries should be avoided. The opening exercises should not consume time required for the preaching of the Word of God. (For suggested forms of service, see Notes, #2, pp. 179, 180.)

Church Outreach (Missionary) Service—The first Sabbath of each month is the Church Outreach (Missionary) Sabbath. This worship service focuses on lay evangelism and may feature plans and activities of various departments. "God has committed to our hands a most sacred work, and we need to meet together to receive instruction, that we may be fitted to perform this work."—6T 32. (See Notes, #4, pp. 181, 182.)

Public Prayer—"Christ impressed upon His disciples the idea that their prayers should be short, expressing just what they wanted, and no more. . . . One or two minutes is long enough for any ordinary prayer."—2T 581.

"Let those who pray and those who speak pronounce their words properly and speak in clear, distinct, even tones. Prayer, if properly offered, is a power for good. It is one of the means used by the Lord to communicate to the people the precious treasures of truth. . . . Let God's people learn how to speak and pray in a way that will properly represent the great truths they possess. Let the testimonies borne and the prayers offered be clear and distinct. Thus God will be glorified."—6T 382.

Supplying Literature on Sabbath—Generally Sabbath is the opportune time for the personal ministries secretary to place literature in the hands of members. Objectionable methods that divert the attention from true worship and reverence should be avoided.

Communion Service

The communion service customarily is celebrated once per quarter. The service includes the ordinance of foot-washing followed by the Lord's Supper. It should be a most sacred and joyous occasion to the congregation, pastor, and elders. The service usually takes place during the worship service but may be scheduled at other times.

Ordinance of Foot-Washing—"Now, having washed the disciples' feet, He said, 'I have given you an example, that ye should do as I have done to you.' In these words Christ was not merely enjoining the practice of hospitality. More was meant than the washing of the feet of guests to remove the dust of travel. Christ was here instituting a religious service. By the act of our Lord this . . . ceremony was made a consecrated ordinance. It was to be observed by the disciples, that they might ever keep in mind His lessons of humility and service.

"This ordinance is Christ's appointed preparation for the sacramental service. While pride, variance, and strife for supremacy are cherished, the heart cannot enter into fellowship with Christ. We are not prepared to receive the communion of His body and His blood. Therefore it was that Jesus appointed the memorial of His humiliation to be first observed."—DA 650.

In the act of washing the disciples' feet, Christ performed a deeper cleansing, that of washing from the heart the stain of sin. The communicants sense an unworthiness to accept the sacred emblems before experiencing the cleansing that makes them "completely clean" (John 13:10). Jesus desired to wash away "alienation, jealousy, and pride from their hearts. . . . Pride and self-seeking create dissension and hatred, but all this Jesus washed away. . . . Looking upon them, Jesus could say, 'Ye are clean.' "—DA 646.

The spiritual experience that lies at the heart of foot-washing lifts it from being a common custom to being a sacred ordinance. It conveys a message of forgiveness, acceptance, assurance, and solidarity, primarily from Christ to the believer, but also between the believers themselves. This message is expressed in an atmosphere of humility.

The Lord's Supper—Angels declare that Jesus, the Redeemer of this world, is holy. Likewise, the symbols representing His body and His blood are holy. Since the Lord Himself selected the deeply meaningful symbols of the unleavened bread and unfermented fruit of the vine and used the simplest of means for washing the disciples' feet, there should be great reluctance to introduce alternative symbols and means, except under emergency conditions, lest the original significance of the service be lost. Likewise in the order of service and the traditional roles played by the pastor, elders, deacons, and deaconesses, there should be caution lest substitution and innovation tend to make common that which is sacred.

The service of the Lord's Supper is just as holy today as it was when instituted by Jesus Christ. Jesus is still present when this sacred ordinance is celebrated. "It is at these, His own appointments, that Christ meets His people, and energizes them by His presence."—DA 656.

Unleavened Bread and Unfermented Wine (Grape Juice)—"Christ is still at the table on which the paschal supper has been spread. The unleavened cakes used at the Passover season are before Him. The Passover wine, untouched by fermentation, is on the table. These emblems Christ employs to represent His own unblemished sacrifice. Nothing corrupted by fermentation, the symbol of sin and death, could represent the 'Lamb without blemish and without spot.' 1 Peter 1:19."—DA 653.

Neither the wine nor the bread contained elements of fermentation because on the evening of the first day of the Hebrew Passover all leaven, or fermentation, had been removed from their dwellings (Ex. 12:15, 19; 13:7). Therefore, only unfermented grape juice and unleavened bread are appropriate for use in the communion service, and great care must be exercised in providing these elements. In isolated areas where grape or raisin juice or concentrate is unavailable, the conference office will advise or assist.

A Memorial of the Crucifixion—"As we receive the bread and wine symbolizing Christ's broken body and spilled blood, we in imagination join in the scene of Communion in the upper chamber. We seem to be passing through the garden consecrated by the agony of Him who bore the sins of the world. We witness the struggle by which our reconciliation with God was obtained. Christ is set forth crucified among us."—DA 661.

A Proclamation of the Second Coming—"The Communion service points to Christ's second coming. It was designed to keep this hope vivid in the minds of the disciples. Whenever they met together to commemorate His death, they recounted how 'he took the cup, and gave thanks, and gave it to them, saying, Drink ye all of it; for this is my blood of the new testament, which is shed for many for the remission of sins. But I say unto you, I will not drink henceforth of this fruit of the vine, until that day when I drink it new with you in my Father's kingdom.' In their tribulation they found comfort in the hope of their Lord's return. Unspeakably precious to them was the thought, 'As often as ye eat this bread, and drink this cup, ye do shew the Lord's death till he come.' 1 Cor. 11:26."—DA 659.

Announcing the Communion Service—The communion service may appropriately be included as part of any Christian worship service. However, to give proper emphasis and make communion available to the greatest number of members, usually it is part of the worship service on the next to the last Sabbath of each quarter.

On the preceding Sabbath an announcement should be made of the service calling attention to the importance of the forthcoming communion, so that all members may prepare their hearts and put aright any unresolved differences they have with one another. When they come to the table of the Lord the following Sabbath, they then can receive the intended blessing. Those absent for the announcement also should be invited to attend.

Conducting the Communion Service—Length of Service—Time is not the most significant factor in the communion service. However, attendance can be improved and the spiritual impact increased by (1) eliminating extraneous items from the worship service on this high day, (2) avoiding delays before and after foot-washing, and (3) having the deaconesses arrange the emblems on the communion table well beforehand.

Preliminaries—The introductory portion of the service should be brief, including only short announcements, a hymn, prayer, offering, and a short sermon before separating for the foot-washing and returning for the Lord's Supper.

Foot-Washing—Each church should have a plan for meeting the needs of its members for the foot-washing service. (See Notes, #5, p. 182.)

Bread and Wine—Following the foot-washing, the congregation comes together once again to partake of the bread and the wine. (See Notes, #6, pp. 182, 183.)

Celebration—Communion should always be a solemn, never somber, experience. Wrongs have been righted, sins have been forgiven, and faith has been reaffirmed. It is a time for celebration. Let the music be bright and joyous. The service should end on a high note, such as with a musical feature or congregational singing, followed by dismissal.

An offering for the poor is often taken as the congregation leaves.

After the service the deacons and deaconesses clear the table, collect the utensils, and respectfully dispose of any remaining emblems. In no case should these emblems be consumed or returned to common use.

Who May Participate—The Church practices open communion. All who have committed their lives to the Savior may participate. Children learn the significance of the service by observing others participating. After receiving formal instruction in baptismal classes and making their commitment to Jesus in baptism, they are thereby prepared to partake in the service themselves.

"Christ's example forbids exclusiveness at the Lord's Supper. It is true that open sin excludes the guilty. This the Holy Spirit plainly teaches. 1 Cor. 5:11. But beyond this none are to pass judgment. God has not left it with men to say who shall present themselves on these occasions. For who can read the heart? Who can distinguish the tares from the wheat? 'Let a man examine himself, and so let him eat of that bread, and drink of that cup.' For 'whosoever shall eat this bread, and drink this cup of the Lord, unworthily, shall be guilty of the body and blood of the Lord.' 'He that eateth and drinketh unworthily, eateth and drinketh damnation to himself, not discerning the Lord's body.' 1 Cor. 11:28, 27, 29. . . . There may come into the company persons who are not in heart servants of truth and holiness, but who may wish to take part in the service. They should not be forbidden. There are witnesses present who were present when Jesus washed the feet of the disciples and of Judas. More than human eyes beheld the scene."—DA 656.

Every Member Should Attend—"None should exclude themselves from the Communion because some who are unworthy may be present. Every disciple is called upon to participate publicly, and thus bear witness that he accepts Christ as a personal Savior. It is at these, His own appointments, that Christ meets His people, and energizes them by His presence. Hearts and hands that are unworthy may even administer the ordinance, yet Christ is there to minister to His children. All who come with their faith fixed upon Him will be greatly blessed. All who neglect these seasons of divine privilege will suffer loss. Of them it may appropriately be said, 'Ye are not all clean.' "—DA 656.

Who May Conduct the Communion Service—The communion service is to be conducted by an ordained pastor or an ordained elder. Deacons, although ordained, cannot conduct the service.

Communion for Those Who Cannot Attend—If members are ill or cannot for other reasons attend the communion service, the pastor or elder, possibly accompanied and assisted by a deacon or deaconess, may conduct a special service in their homes.

Prayer Meeting

Prayer Meetings Should Be Interesting—"The prayer meetings should be the most interesting gatherings that are held, but these are frequently poorly managed. Many attend preaching, but neglect the prayer meeting. Here, again, thought is required. Wisdom should be sought of God, and plans should be laid to conduct the meetings so that they will be interesting and attractive. The people hunger for the bread of life. If they find it at the prayer meeting they will go there to receive it.

"Long, prosy talks and prayers are out of place anywhere, and especially in the social [prayer] meeting. Those who are forward and ever ready to speak are allowed to crowd out the testimony of the timid and retiring. Those who are most superficial generally have the most to say. Their prayers are long and mechanical. They weary the angels and the people who listen to them. Our prayers should be short and right to the point. Let the long, tiresome petitions be left for the closet, if any have such to offer. Let the Spirit of God into your hearts, and it will sweep away all dry formality."—4T 70, 71.

More than ordinary efforts should be made to assure the success of the prayer meeting. The meeting should begin on time, even if only two or three persons are present. There should be a short, 15- to 20-minute Scripture study or presentation from the Spirit of Prophecy, followed by prayer, testimonies, and a benediction.

Vary the plan of the service from week to week.

If members are unable to assemble at the usual place for prayer meeting, home meetings may be of great benefit.

Business Meetings

The local church operates within defined roles in Seventh-day Adventist Church structure. Within the context of those roles, the business meeting is the constituency meeting of the local church. (See p. 27) Members in regular standing are encouraged to attend and are entitled to vote. A member under censure has no right to participate by voice or vote.

Business meetings shall be held at least once a year. The pastor, or the board in consultation with and support of the pastor, calls the meeting. Business meetings typically are announced a week or two in advance at the regular Sabbath worship service, with detail as to time and place. The pastor, an elder arranged by the pastor, or, in some cases, the conference president, serves as chairperson of the business meeting.

Each church decides what the quorum will be for future meetings.

Votes by proxy or letter are not permitted.

Major items should be decided at a regular or specially called business meeting.

The business meeting has authority over the board and may delegate responsibilities to the board in addition to those already assigned by the *Church Manual*. (See pp. 129-132.)

The business meeting agenda should include reports about the work of the church. At least once a year the agenda should include reports covering church activities. Based on those reports, a proposed plan of action for the next year, including an annual budget, should be presented for approval. When possible, reports and plans for the next year should be presented in writing. (See Notes, #7, pp. 183, 184.)

In order to maintain a spirit of cooperation between the church and conference, the church shall secure counsel from conference officers on all major matters.

Conference and union officers (president, secretary, treasurer) or their designee may attend without vote (unless granted by the church) any business meeting of any church in their territory. An action to allow voting is not required if the officer is currently a member of that congregation.

Church Board and Its Meetings

Definition and Function—Every church must have a functioning board whose members have been elected during a church business meeting. Its chief concern is having an active discipleship plan in place, which includes both the spiritual nurture of the church and the work of planning and fostering evangelism.

Included in church board responsibilities are:

1. An active discipleship plan.
2. Evangelism in all of its phases.
3. Spiritual nurturing and mentoring of members.
4. Maintenance of doctrinal purity.
5. Upholding of Christian standards.
6. Recommending changes in church membership.
7. Oversight of church finances.
8. Protection and care of church properties.
9. Coordination of church departments.

The gospel commission of Jesus tells us that making disciples, which includes baptizing and teaching, is the primary function of the church (Matt. 28:18-20). It is, therefore, also the primary function of the board, which serves as the chief committee of the church. When the board devotes its first interests and highest energies to involving every member in proclaiming the good news and making disciples, most problems are alleviated or prevented, and a strong, positive influence is felt in the spiritual life and growth of members.

Spiritual Nurture—Christ's love for the Church needs to be manifested within the Church by His followers. True discipleship entails not only Biblical teaching (Matt. 28:20), but also a passionate commitment to loving our fellow believers unconditionally. This was the heart of Christ's message to His disciples as He faced the cross (John 15:9-13). Christ's command to them applies to us: that we "love one another." Ellen G. White's powerful insight into this historical scene is still vital for us: "This love is the evidence of their discipleship."—DA 677, 678.

Therefore, it is one of the primary functions of the board to ensure that members are nurtured and mentored in a personal, dynamic relationship with Jesus Christ.

Discipleship—The purpose of the Church as the body of Christ is to intentionally disciple members, so that they continue in an active and fruitful relationship with Christ and His Church.

Discipleship is based on an ongoing, lifelong relationship with Jesus. The believer commits to "abiding in Christ" (John 15:8), to being trained for fruitful discipleship by sharing Jesus with others, as well as to leading other members to also be faithful disciples.

The Church, individually and collectively, shares responsibility for ensuring that every church member remains part of the body of Christ.

Membership—The board is elected by the members at the time of the regular election officers. (See pp. 71, 72.) In addition to conference-appointed pastors, the church should elect a representative board that includes the following officers:

Elders
Head deacon
Head deaconess
Treasurer
Clerk
Interest coordinator
Adventist Community Services leader or Dorcas Society leader
Adventist Men's coordinator
Adventist Youth Ministries leader
Adventurer Club director
Ambassador Club leader
Bible school coordinator
Children's ministries leader
Church music coordinator
Communication committee chairperson or communication secretary
Education secretary/church school principal or head teacher
Family ministries leader
Health ministries leader
Home and School Association leader
Pathfinder Club director
Personal ministries leader and secretary
Public Campus Ministries leader/coordinator
Publishing ministries coordinator Religious liberty leader
Sabbath School superintendent

Stewardship ministries leader

Women's ministries leader

Young adults leader

In some cases, depending on the size of the membership, the board may not include all of this list or may add additional members. The pastor appointed by the conference to serve the church always is a member of the board.

Officers—The chairperson of the board is the conference-appointed pastor. If the pastor prefers not to act in this capacity or is unable to be present, he/she may arrange for an elder to preside as chairperson.

The clerk serves as secretary of the board and is responsible for recording, presenting, and preserving the minutes of the meetings.

Meetings—Because the work of the board is vital to the life, health, and growth of the church, it is recommended that it meet at least once each month, more frequently if needed. It is well to fix the monthly meeting time for the same week and the same day each month.

The board meeting is announced at the regular Sabbath worship service, and all board members are urged to attend.

Each church should determine at a business meeting the number of board members who must be present to constitute a quorum at future meetings.

Votes by proxy or letter are not permitted.

Work of the Board—The board is responsible to: 1. Ensure that there is an active, ongoing discipleship plan in place, which includes both spiritual nurture and outreach ministries. This is the most important item for the board's attention.

2. Study membership lists and initiate plans for reconnecting (reclaiming) members who have separated from the church.

3. Train local church leadership in how to encourage intentional spiritual growth in themselves and others.

4. Evangelize the outreach (missionary) territory of the church. Once each quarter an entire meeting should be devoted to plans for evangelism. The board will study conference recommendations for evangelistic programs and methods and how they can be implemented locally. The pastor and the board will initiate and develop plans for public evangelistic meetings.

5.   Coordinate outreach programs for all church departments, although each department develops its plans for outreach within its own sphere. To avoid conflict in timing, competition in securing volunteers, and to achieve maximum beneficial results, coordination is essential. Before completing and announcing plans for any program, each department should submit its plans to the board for approval. The departments also report to the board on the progress and results of their outreach programs. The board may suggest how departmental programs can contribute to the preparation, conduct, and follow-up of a public evangelistic campaign.

6.   Encourage the personal ministries department to enlist all members and children in some form of personal outreach (missionary) service. Training classes should be conducted in various lines of outreach ministry.

7.   Encourage the interest coordinator to ensure that every interest is personally and promptly followed up by assigned laypersons.

8.   Encourage each department to report at least quarterly to the board and to members at business meetings or in Sabbath meetings in regards to spiritual nurture and evangelism.

9.   Receive regular reports. The board should consider details of church business and receive regular reports of the treasurer on the church's finances. The board should study the membership record and inquire into the spiritual standing of all members and provide for visits to sick, discouraged, or backslidden members. Other officers should periodically report.

10. Promote Adventist education.

Committees of the Board—The board should permit no other business to interfere with planning for evangelism. Should other business be too time-consuming, the board should appoint committees to care for specific areas of church business, such as finance or church building projects. Such committees will then make recommendations to the board. (See Notes, #8, p. 184.)

Finance Committee

Each church should have a mission-driven, broadly-based consultative financial planning and budgeting process with a committee structure that can give detailed review to the ongoing financial planning and budgeting. In some cases, this may take the form of a finance committee. In other cases, in smaller churches, this process may be handled directly by the church board. If the church establishes a separate committee for this purpose, the responsibilities should include reviewing budget requests and the review of the annual operating budget as well as a review of the financial position of the church as reflected in the financial statements. The approval of the budget and the review of the financial statement shall then be recommended to the church board and onward to the business meeting of the church for action.

School Board Meetings

The church school is usually supervised by a church school board. The church elects a chairperson to preside over meetings and a secretary to keep records of meetings and actions. This board should meet at regular times. Special meetings may be called by the chairperson. Some churches prefer to have the church board, or a subcommittee of the church board, also serve as the school board. (See also pp. 90-92.)

Home and School Association Meetings

The Home and School Association should meet monthly and coordinate the activities of home, school, and church. Attention should be given to the education of parents, as well as to assisting the school to obtain needed resources, such as room parents, books, teaching materials, and equipment. Materials to assist Home and School leaders are available through the conference education department. (See also p. 90.)

Youth Meetings

Leaders of the church's various youth groups should schedule regular meetings that involve the church's young people in meaningful activities that will tie them closer to the church and train them for useful service. (See also pp. 104-109.)

Senior Youth Ministries Meetings (Ambassadors and Young Adults)—Senior Youth Ministries meetings should convene on a regular schedule and focus on developing the spiritual, mental, emotional, and physical characteristics of the church's youth. Meetings also provide Christian social interaction and witnessing programs supporting the soul-winning plans of the church. For resources, see Notes #9, p. 184.

Public Campus Ministries Meetings—Where the church has appointed a Public Campus Ministries director/coordinator, meetings should be organized to care for the special needs of public college/university students in consultation with and support of the Adventist Youth Ministries Committee.

Junior Youth Ministries Meetings (Adventurers and Pathfinders)—Junior Youth Ministries meetings are similar in purpose to Senior Youth Ministries, but involve junior youth. Adventurer Club meetings provide specialized programs for primary/early school-age children designed to complement and strengthen parental involvement in early childhood development, while Pathfinder Club meetings provide specialized indoor and outdoor activities for the holistic development of children from 10 to15 years old. Meetings and other activities are to be carried out according to conference policies as outlined in the club manuals and in coordination with other youth-related and family-related organizations of the church.

CHAPTER 11

Finance

The biblical plan for the support of the work of God is by the tithes and offerings of His people. The Lord says, "Bring all the tithes into the storehouse, that there may be food in My house" (Mal. 3:10). The Church has followed this plan from its earliest days.

"The system of tithes and offerings was intended to impress the minds of men with a great truth—that God is the source of every blessing to His creatures, and that to Him man's gratitude is due for the good gifts of His providence."—PP 525.

"Tithes and offerings for God are an acknowledgment of His claim on us by creation, and they are also an acknowledgment of His claim by redemption. Because all our power is derived from Christ, these offerings are to flow from us to God. They are to keep ever before us the claim of redemption, the greatest of all claims, and the one that involves every other."—6T 479.

"The tithe is sacred, reserved by God for Himself. It is to be brought into His treasury to be used to sustain the gospel laborers in their work."—9T 249.

"He has given His people a plan for raising sums sufficient to make the enterprise self-sustaining. God's plan in the tithing system is beautiful in its simplicity and equality. All may take hold of it in faith and courage, for it is divine in its origin. In it are combined simplicity and utility. . . . Every man, woman, and youth may become a treasurer for the Lord and may be an agent to meet the demands upon the treasury. Says the apostle: 'Let every one of you lay by him in store, as God hath prospered him.' "—3T 388, 389.

"God has made the proclamation of the gospel dependent upon the labors and the gifts of His people. Voluntary offerings and the tithe constitute the revenue of the Lord's work. Of the means entrusted to man, God claims a certain portion—the tenth. He leaves all free to say whether or not they will give more than this."—AA 74.

"God has given special direction as to the use of the tithe. He does not design that His work shall be crippled for want of means. . . . The portion that God has reserved for Himself is not to be diverted to any other purpose than that which He has specified. Let none feel at liberty to retain their tithe, to use according to their own judgment. They are not to use it for themselves in an emergency, nor to apply it as they see fit, even in what they may regard as the Lord's work."—9T 247.

Stewardship

Christians are God's stewards, entrusted with His goods and, as His partners, responsible to manage them in harmony with His guidelines and principles. The divine counsel is that as His stewards, we are to "be found faithful" (1 Cor. 4:2). Though the question of stewardship covers many aspects of Christian life and experience, without doubt the stewardship of our means is vitally important. It concerns the entire Church family and involves our recognition of the sovereignty of God, His ownership of all things, and the bestowal of His grace upon our hearts.

While this aspect of Christian stewardship concerns our material possessions, it nevertheless reacts upon our Christian experience. The Lord requires certain things of us, in order that He may do certain things for us. Our yielding obedience to what our heavenly Father requires places this phase of stewardship upon a high spiritual plane. He does not arbitrarily demand either that we serve Him or that we recognize Him with our gifts. But He has so arranged that when we work in harmony with Him in these things there will flow to our own hearts great spiritual blessings.

"God desires all His stewards to be exact in following divine arrangements. They are not to offset the Lord's plans by performing some deed of charity or giving some gift or some offering when or how they, the human agents, shall see fit. It is a very poor policy for men to seek to improve on God's plan, and invent a makeshift, averaging up their good impulses on this and that occasion, and offsetting them against God's requirements. God calls upon all to give their influence to His own arrangement."—9T 248.

Tithe

In recognition of the biblical plan and the solemn privilege and responsibility that rest upon members as children of God and members of His body, the Church, all are encouraged to faithfully return a tithe, one tenth of their increase or personal income, into the denomination's treasury.

Tithe shall not be used in any way by the local church, but held in trust and remitted to the conference treasurer. Thus tithe from all the churches flows into the conference treasury, and percentages are forwarded to the next-higher level in accordance with General Conference and division working policies to meet the expenses of conducting the work of God in their respective spheres of responsibility and activity.

These policies have been developed for the gathering and disbursing of funds in all the world and for the conducting of the business affairs of the cause. The financial and business aspects of the work are of great importance. They cannot be separated from the proclamation of the message of salvation. They are indeed an integral part of it.

Systematic Benevolence and Unity—The financial plan of the Church serves a larger purpose than appears in its financial and statistical reports. The system of sharing the funds with the world fields, as outlined by General Conference Working Policy, serves a wonderful purpose of unifying the Church's spiritual work throughout the world.

How Tithe Is to Be Used—Tithe is held sacred for the work of the ministry, for Bible teaching, and for the support of conference administration in the care of the churches and of field outreach (missionary) endeavors. Tithe shall not be spent on other work, on paying church or institutional debts, or on building programs, except as approved under General Conference *Working Policy*. For more information on the use of tithe, see Notes, #1, p. 184.

"A very plain, definite message has been given to me for our people. I am bidden to tell them that they are making a mistake in applying the tithe to various objects which, though good in themselves, are not the object to which the Lord has said that the tithe should be applied. Those who make this use of the tithe are departing from the Lord's arrangement. God will judge for these things."—9T 248.

How Tithe Is Handled—Tithe is the Lord's and is to be brought as an act of worship to the conference treasury through the church in which the person's membership is held. Where unusual circumstances exist, members should consult with conference officers.

Church and Conference Officers to Set Example—Elders and other officers, as well as the pastor and conference and institutional employees, are expected to set good leadership examples by returning tithe. No one shall be continued as either a church officer or conference employee who does not conform to this standard of leadership.

Offerings

In addition to the tithe, Scripture emphasizes our obligation to bring offerings to the Lord. The withholding of offerings is classed with withholding tithe and is called robbery (Mal. 3:8). Since the Church's earliest days, members have given liberal offerings that have blessed and prospered God's work.

In addition to the traditional calendar of offerings program, where each offering taken is for a specific purpose, the General Conference has approved the combined offering system and the personal giving plan. The division committee is authorized to determine which plan(s) will be used in its territory.

Sabbath School Offerings—The Church's most widely used and successful method of regular systematic giving is through Sabbath School offerings, which are devoted to world mission work.

Other Offerings—Other offerings are taken from time to time for world mission work and for general and local projects. When any offering is taken, all money collected, unless otherwise indicated by the donor, shall be counted as part of that particular offering.

Special Gifts to Fields—The financial support of the worldwide work of the Church is based on the budget system. Appropriations are made to the various fields on the basis of budgeted needs. This is a fair and equitable method of distributing the funds.

Where special gifts outside the regular budget plan are made to a particular field, a disparity is created to the disadvantage of other fields. If such gifts are given for the purpose of starting new work, the work thus started may languish when the special gift is used up, or it may have to be included in the budget for its future support. Thus other fields, with perhaps greater needs but without the opportunity of making them known, would be deprived of their equitable part of general funds that would be diverted to the work started by special gifts.

History has proved the wisdom of having members generously and loyally give their offerings and gifts through the accepted channels and knowing that every field shares in the benefits of their giving.

Assisting the Poor and Needy—Offerings for the poor and needy are taken to assist the members who require help. A reserve fund should be kept for such emergency cases. In addition, the church should take a benevolent attitude toward all in need, and the board may make appropriations from this fund to assist the church's health and welfare work for families in the community.

Church Budget for Local Expenses—The most satisfactory method of providing for church expenses is the budget plan. Before the beginning of the new budget year, the board should prepare a budget of expenses for church activities during the next year. The budget should include all income and expenses, including those related to all departments. It should provide for such projected costs as utilities, insurance, maintenance, janitor service, funds for the poor and needy, and church school expense. (See Notes, #2, p. 185, for sample budget.)

The budget should be presented to the church for its study and adoption, and for plans to assure that funds shall be provided to balance the budget during the coming year. Funds to meet the church expense budget may be raised by offerings or subscriptions. Members should be urged to support their local church in proportion to their financial circumstances.

General Financial Counsel

Regulation of Soliciting Funds—The following are regulations for soliciting funds:

1. No conference, church, or institution, without special counsel and arrangement, shall plan work requiring solicitation of funds from outside its territory. Any solicitation within its territory shall be in harmony with local, union, division, and General Conference policies. No authority is granted to denominational employees representing special interests in one part of the field to solicit help in any other part of the field or in any other conference without arrangement with and written authorization from conference officers where the fund-raising would take place.

2. The following principles protect churches from unauthorized, fraudulent, and undenominational solicitation:

   a.   Pastors and officers shall not grant the privilege of the pulpit to persons for fund-raising who have not been recognized or recommended by the conference. (See pp. 120, 121.) No permission shall be granted to solicit funds either publicly or privately without such recognition.

   b.   All funds contributed for any cause in response to appeals shall be passed through regular church channels.

c.   Conference and church officers shall take such steps as may be necessary to prevent unauthorized or illegal public solicitation.

3.   No campaign other than the Annual Appeal (Ingathering or equivalent appeal), which involves using Appeal literature and containers with authorized Appeal labels, shall be conducted for the solicitation of money for either home or overseas mission work. Unions and conferences should prevent violations of this regulation.

4.   Interdivision employees visiting their home churches or otherwise communicating with their home bases are asked to solicit funds only for enterprises included in the budget of appropriations, working in cooperation with churches and conferences to raise the funds required to meet the appropriations on which our world mission work depends. All such funds shall be passed through regular channels.

Questionable Methods for Raising Funds—The local church should take a strong stand against questionable methods for raising money.

"When money is raised for religious purposes, to what means do many churches resort? To bazaars, suppers, fancy fairs, even to lotteries and like devices. Often the place set apart for God's worship is desecrated by feasting and drinking, buying, selling, and merrymaking. Respect for the house of God and reverence for His worship are lessened in the minds of the youth. The barriers of self-restraint are weakened. Selfishness, appetite, the love of display, are appealed to, and they strengthen as they are indulged."—9T 91.

"As God's work extends, calls for help will come more and more frequently. . . . If professing Christians would faithfully bring to God their tithes and offerings, His treasury would be full. There would then be no occasion to resort to fairs, lotteries, or parties of pleasure to secure funds for the support of the gospel."—AA 338.

Tithes and Offerings Not a Personal Trust Fund—Tithes and offerings donated by members to the Church do not create a trust fund for the future benefit of the givers. These funds shall be used for the current purposes for which they are given.

Financing Building Plans—Churches considering the purchase or erection of church or other buildings, or incurring debt of any kind, should counsel with conference officers before undertaking such financial obligations. In the purchase or building of church properties, in no case shall commitments be made or building operations begun until approval has been given by the conference and union committees. These committees will approve only after they have assured themselves that the financial arrangements conform to established policies. In giving financial counsel, the conference committee should consider the size of the congregation, its financial strength, and the location of the building.

Handling and Accounting for Funds—The gathering and handling of funds for the Lord's work is a sacred responsibility. The proper channel through which these funds flow is first from members to the local church, where the treasurer receives the funds. (See pp. 82-86.) The treasurer disburses funds intended for local church purposes. The treasurer holds in trust and passes on to the conference treasurer funds intended for conference or general purposes. The treasurer of the local church works under the direction of the board. Treasurers of any level (local church, conference, union, or division/General Conference) do not act independently. They disburse funds only by action or authority of responsible committees.

Auditing—Every set of accounting records, from those of the local church to those of the General Conference, are subject to audit by auditors appointed for the purpose. This rule, which also applies to every denominationally affiliated institution, provides the maximum of safety in the handling of funds. (See pp. 85, 86.)

CHAPTER 12

Standards of Christian Living

High Calling of God in Christ Jesus

The Christian's life is not a slight modification or improvement, but a complete transformation of nature. This means a death to self and sin and a resurrection to a new life as a new person in Christ Jesus.

The heart of the Christian becomes the dwelling place of Christ by faith. This is brought about by "the contemplation of Christ, beholding Christ, ever cherishing the dear Savior as our very best and honored Friend, so that we would not in any action grieve and offend Him"—TM 387. Thus Christians "have the companionship of the divine presence," and as we realize that presence, "our thoughts are brought into captivity to Jesus Christ" (TM 388) and our habits made to conform to the divine standard.

We should bear in mind that "as a shield from temptation and an inspiration to purity and truth, no other influence can equal the sense of God's presence."—Ed 255.

"No part of our conduct escapes observation. We cannot hide our ways from the Most High. . . . Every act, every word, every thought, is as distinctly marked as though there were only one person in the whole world, and the attention of heaven were centered upon him."—PP 217, 218.

God's love extends to everyone, and to His children in particular. His ear is ever open to the appeals of His people, those who have turned from the world and given themselves to Him. Out of this sacred relationship grows a respect and a reverence that is manifested every day and everywhere.

As Christians we are members of the royal family, children of the heavenly King. Therefore, we should say no word and perform no act that would bring dishonor upon "that noble name by which you are called" (James 2:7). We are reformers. In every phase of life we should "study carefully the divine-human character and constantly inquire, 'What would Jesus do were He in my place?' This should be the measurement of our duty."—MH 491.

Through the remnant Church God will demonstrate to the entire universe the adequacy of the gospel to save men and women from the power of sin. As members of that Church we should emphasize again the great Bible standards and renew allegiance to these God-given principles. We should come up to the high standards of the Christian life and be separated from the world. To this end we would heed the Lord's admonition: "Do not love the world or the things in the world. If anyone loves the world, the love of the Father is not in him" (1 John 2:15).

Bible Study and Prayer

Spiritual life is maintained by spiritual food. We must maintain the habit of devotional Bible study and prayer if we are to perfect holiness. In a time when a flood of communication pours forth from the printed page, radio, television, the Internet, and other modern mass media, when thousands of voices plead for a hearing, we must close our eyes and our ears to much that seeks entrance to our minds and devote ourselves to God's Book, the Book of all books, the Book of life—the Bible. If we cease to be the people of the Book, we are lost, and our mission has failed. Only as we daily talk to God in prayer and listen to His voice can we hope to live the life that is "hidden with Christ in God" (Col. 3:3) and finish His work.

Prayer is a two-way conversation in which we listen to and talk to God. "Prayer is the opening of the heart to God as to a friend."—SC 93. "Through sincere prayer we are brought into connection with the mind of the Infinite," and "without unceasing prayer and diligent watching we are in danger of growing careless and of deviating from the right path."—SC 97, 95.

The home is the cornerstone of the Church. A Christian home is a house of prayer. "Fathers and mothers, however pressing your business, do not fail to gather your family around God's altar. . . . Those who would live patient, loving, cheerful lives must pray."—MH 393.

Community Relationships

While our "citizenship is in heaven, from which we also eagerly wait for the Savior, the Lord Jesus Christ" (Phil. 3:20), we are yet in the world as an integral part of human society and must share with our fellow citizens certain responsibilities in the common problems of life. Wherever we live, as children of God we should be recognized as outstanding citizens in our Christian integrity and in working for the common good.

While our highest responsibility is to the Church and the gospel commission, we should support by our service and our means, as far as possible and consistent with our beliefs, efforts for social order and betterment. Even though we must stand apart from political and social strife, we should always, quietly and firmly, maintain an uncompromising stand for justice and right in civic affairs, along with full adherence to our religious convictions. It is our sacred responsibility to be loyal citizens of the nations to which we belong, rendering "to Caesar the things that are Caesar's, and to God the things that are God's" (Matt. 22:21).

Sabbathkeeping

The Sabbath is a token of God's love to humanity. It is a memorial of God's power in the original creation and also a sign of His power to re-create and sanctify our lives (Eze. 20:12), and its observance is an evidence of our loyalty to Him and of our fellowship with Him.

The Sabbath holds a special place in our lives. The seventh day of the week, from sunset Friday to sunset Saturday (Lev. 23:32), is a gift from God, a sign of His grace in time. It is a privilege, a special appointment with the One who loves us and whom we love, a sacred time set aside by God's eternal law, a day of delight for worshipping God and sharing with others (Isa. 58:13). We welcome the Sabbath with joy and gratitude.

"The Sabbath—oh!—make it the sweetest, the most blessed day of the whole week."—FLB 36.

"The Sabbath . . . is God's time, not ours; when we trespass upon it we are stealing from God. . . . God has given us the whole of six days in which to do our work, and has reserved only one to Himself. This should be a day of blessing to us—a day when we should lay aside all our secular matters and center our thoughts upon God and heaven. . . .

"We are not to teach our children that they must not be happy on the Sabbath, that it is wrong to walk out of doors. Oh, no. Christ led His disciples out by the lakeside on the Sabbath day and taught them. His sermons on the Sabbath were not always preached within enclosed walls."—HP 152.

"God's love has set a limit to the demands of toil. Over the Sabbath He places His merciful hand. In His own day He preserves for the family opportunity for communion with Him, with nature, and with one another."—Ed 251.

The Sabbath hours belong to God and are to be used for Him alone. Our own pleasure, words, business, and thoughts should find no place in the observance of the Lord's day (Isa. 58:13). Let us gather in the family circle at sunset and welcome the Sabbath with prayer and song, and let us close the day with prayer and expressions of gratitude for His wondrous love. The Sabbath is a special day for worship in our homes and churches, a day of joy to ourselves and our children, a day in which we can learn more of God through the Bible and the great lesson book of nature. It is a time we can visit the sick and work for the salvation of souls. We should lay aside the ordinary affairs of the six working days and perform no unnecessary work. We should not let secular media occupy our time on God's holy day.

"The Sabbath is not intended to be a period of useless inactivity. The law forbids secular labor on the rest day of the Lord; the toil that gains a livelihood must cease; no labor for worldly pleasure or profit is lawful upon that day; but as God ceased His labor of creating, and rested upon the Sabbath and blessed it, so man is to leave the occupations of his daily life, and devote those sacred hours to healthful rest, to worship, and to holy deeds."—DA 207.

A program of activities in harmony with the spirit of true Sabbathkeeping will make this blessed day the happiest and best of all the week for ourselves and for our children—a veritable foretaste of our heavenly rest.

Reverence in the Place of Worship

Christians who appreciate God's omnipotence, His holiness, and His love will always manifest a spirit of deep reverence for God, His Word, and His worship. "Humility and reverence should characterize the deportment of all who come into the presence of God."—PP 252. We will recognize that "the hour and place of prayer are sacred, because God is there."—GW 178. We will come to the house of worship, not carelessly, but in the spirit of meditation and prayer, and will avoid unnecessary conversation.

As parents we should reverently instruct our children how they should behave in "the house of God" (1 Tim. 3:15). Faithful instruction and discipline of youth at home, Sabbath School, and church regarding reverence for God and His worship will go far in holding their loyalty in afteryears.

Pastors who sense the sacredness of God's service will, by example, instruction, and conduct in the pulpit, foster reverence, simplicity, good order, and decorum in the church.

Health and Temperance

Our bodies are the temple of the Holy Spirit (1 Cor. 6:19). "Both mental and spiritual vigor are in great degree dependent upon physical strength and activity; whatever promotes physical health promotes the development of a strong mind and a well-balanced character."—Ed 195.

For this reason, we live intelligently in accordance with health principles of physical exercise, respiration, sunshine, pure air, use of water, sleep, and rest. By conviction we choose to eat healthfully, wear suitable clothing, practice cleanliness, engage in proper recreation, and freely choose to follow the principles of health, self-control, and wholesome diet. Therefore we abstain from all forms of alcohol, tobacco, and addictive drugs. We strive to preserve our physical and psychological balance by avoiding any excess.

Health reform and the teaching of health and temperance are inseparable parts of the Church's message. Instruction came to us through the Lord's messenger "that those who are keeping His commandments must be brought into sacred relationship to Himself, and that by temperance in eating and drinking they must keep mind and body in the most favorable condition for service."—CH 132. Also, "it is the Lord's design that the restoring influence of health reform shall be a part of the last great effort to proclaim the gospel message."—MM 259.

We belong to God, body, soul, and spirit. It is therefore our religious duty to observe the laws of health, both for our own well-being and happiness and for more efficient service to God and society. We must keep our appetites under control. God has furnished us with a liberal variety of foods sufficient to satisfy every dietary need. "Fruits, grains, and vegetables, prepared in a simple way, . . . make, with milk or cream, the most healthful diet."—CD 92.

When we practice the principles of healthful living, we will not feel the need for stimulants. Nature's law forbids our use of intoxicants and narcotics of any kind. From the early days of this movement abstinence from the use of liquor and tobacco has been a condition of membership. (See pp. 46, 48, 62, 93, 170.)

God has given us great light on the principles of health, and modern scientific research has abundantly verified these principles.

Dress

As Seventh-day Adventist Christians we have been called out from the world. Our religion must have a molding influence on all our activities. Our habits must stem from principle and not from the example of the world. Customs and fashions may change, but principles of right conduct remain the same. Early in our history Ellen G. White wrote that the purpose of Christian dress is "to protect the people of God from the corrupting influence of the world, as well as to promote physical and moral health."—4T 634. She also counsels that we should avoid gaudy display and profuse ornamentation, fads and extreme fashions, particularly those transgressing the laws of modesty, and that our clothing should be, when possible, "of good quality, of becoming colors, and suited for service" "rather than display." Our attire should be characterized by modesty, "beauty," "grace," and "appropriateness of natural simplicity."—MYP 351, 352.

The people of God should always be found among the conservatives in dress, and will not let "the dress question fill the mind."—Ev 273.

"To dress plainly, abstaining from display of jewelry and ornaments of every kind, is in keeping with our faith."—3T 366. It is clearly taught in the Scriptures that the wearing of jewelry is contrary to the will of God. The apostle Paul admonishes us to dress ourselves "in modest apparel, with propriety and moderation, not with braided hair or gold or pearls or costly clothing" (1 Tim. 2:9). The wearing of ornaments of jewelry is a bid for attention not in keeping with Christian self-forgetfulness.

In some countries and cultures the custom of wearing the wedding ring is considered imperative, having become, in the minds of the people, a criterion of virtue, and hence it is not regarded as an ornament. Under such circumstances we do not condemn the practice.

Let us remember that it is not outward adornment that expresses true Christian character, but "the hidden person of the heart, with the incorruptible beauty of a gentle and quiet spirit, which is very precious in the sight of God" (1 Peter 3:3, 4). We should avoid the use of cosmetics not in keeping with good taste and the principles of Christian modesty.

We should observe cleanliness and Christlike deportment as we seek at all times to please and rightly represent Christ our Lord. Christian parents by example, instruction, and authority should lead their sons and daughters to attire themselves modestly, and thus win the respect and confidence of those who know them. Let us consider ourselves well dressed only when we meet the demands of modesty by wearing tasteful, conservative clothing.

Simplicity

Simplicity has been a fundamental feature of the Church from its beginning. We must continue to be a people called to live a simple life. Increase of pomp in religion always parallels a decline in spiritual power. As "the life of Jesus presented a marked contrast" to the display and ostentation of His time (Ed 77), so the simplicity and power of our message must be in marked contrast to the worldly display of our day. The Lord condemns "needless, extravagant expenditure of money to gratify pride and love of display."—TM 179. In harmony with these principles, simplicity and economy should characterize our graduating exercises, our weddings, and all other church services.

Modern Media

Like our bodies, our inner beings need wholesome nourishment for renewal and strengthening (2 Cor. 4:6). Our minds are the measure of our persons. Food for our minds is of the utmost importance in developing character and in carrying out our life's purposes. For this reason we should carefully evaluate our mental habits. What we choose to read, hear, and watch, whether by book or magazine, radio or television, the Internet, or other modern media shapes and impacts our character.

Books and other literature are among the most valuable means of education and culture, but these must be well chosen and rightly used. There is a wealth of good literature, but equally there is a flood of literature, often in most attractive guise, that damages minds and morals. The tales of wild adventure and of moral laxness, whether fact or fiction, however presented, are unfit for Christians of any age.

"Those who indulge the habit of racing through an exciting story are simply crippling their mental strength and disqualifying their minds for vigorous thought and research."—CT 135. Along with other evil results from the habit of reading fiction, we are told that "it unfits the soul to contemplate the great problems of duty and destiny" and "creates a distaste for life's practical duties."—CT 383.

Radio, television, and the Internet have changed the whole atmosphere of our modern world and have brought us within easy contact with the life, thought, and activities of the entire globe. They can be great educational agencies through which we can enlarge our knowledge of world events and enjoy important discussions and the best in music.

Unfortunately, however, modern mass media also can bring to their audiences almost continuous theatrical and other performances with influences that are neither wholesome nor uplifting. If we are not discriminating, they will bring sordid programs right into our homes.

Safety for ourselves and our children is found in a determination, by God's help, to follow the admonition of the apostle Paul: "Finally . . . whatever things are true . . . noble . . . just . . . pure . . . lovely . . . of good report, if there is any virtue and if there is anything praiseworthy—meditate on these things" (Phil. 4:8).

Recreation and Entertainment

Recreation is a purposeful refreshing of the powers of body and mind. A vigorous, wholesome mind will not require worldly amusement but will find a renewal of strength in good recreation.

"Many of the amusements popular in the world today, even with those who claim to be Christians, tend to the same end as did those of the heathen. There are indeed few among them that Satan does not turn to account in destroying souls. Through the drama he has worked for ages to excite passion and glorify vice. The opera, with its fascinating display and bewildering music, the masquerade, the dance, the card table, Satan employs to break down the barriers of principle and open the door to sensual indulgence. In every gathering for pleasure where pride is fostered or appetite indulged, where one is led to forget God and lose sight of eternal interests, there Satan is binding his chains about the soul."—PP 459, 460. (See p. 170.)

We must avoid anything that dramatizes, graphically presents, or suggests the sins and crimes of humanity—murder, adultery, robbery, and similar evils, which to a large degree are responsible for the breakdown of morality. Instead, we should find delight in God's great world of nature and in the romance of human agencies and divine workings.

Social dancing is another form of amusement with an evil influence. "The amusement of dancing . . . is a school of depravity, a fearful curse to society."—MYP 399. (See 2 Cor. 6:15-18; 1 John 2:15-17; James 4:4; 2 Tim. 2:19-22; Eph. 5:8-11; Col. 3:5-10.)

Recreation is essential. But instead of joining the multitudes who are "lovers of pleasure rather than lovers of God" (2 Tim. 3:4), we should endeavor to make our friendships and recreations both Christ-centered and church-centered.

Music

"Music was made to serve a holy purpose, to lift the thoughts to that which is pure, noble, and elevating, and to awaken in the soul devotion and gratitude to God."—PP 594. Jesus "held communion with heaven in song."—DA 73.

Music is one of the highest arts. Good music not only gives us pleasure but elevates our minds and cultivates our finest qualities. God often has used spiritual songs to touch the hearts of sinners and lead to repentance.

On the contrary, debased music breaks down morality and draws us away from our relationship with God.

We should exercise great care in the choice of music in our homes, social gatherings, schools, and churches. Any melody partaking of the nature of jazz, rock, or related hybrid forms, or any language expressing foolish or trivial sentiments, will be shunned. (See pp. 94, 99, 149.)

Conclusion

Standing amid the perils of the last days, bearing the responsibility of speedily carrying the last offer of salvation to the world, and facing a judgment that will culminate in the establishment of universal righteousness, let us consecrate ourselves body, soul, and spirit to God, determining to maintain the high standards of living that must characterize those who wait for the return of their Lord.

CHAPTER 13

Marriage, Divorce, and Remarriage

Social Relationships

God gives us the social instinct for our pleasure and benefit. "By mutual contact minds receive polish and refinement; by social intercourse, acquaintances are formed and friendships contracted which result in a unity of heart and an atmosphere of love which is pleasing in the sight of heaven."—6T 172.

Proper association of the sexes is beneficial to both. Such association should be conducted upon a high plane and with regard for the social conventions that have been prescribed for our protection. It is the purpose of Satan to pervert every good thing, and the perversion of the best often leads to that which is worst.

Today the ideals that make these social relationships safe and happy are breaking down to an alarming degree. Under the influence of passion unrestrained by moral and religious principle, the association of the sexes has to a large extent degenerated into freedom and license, sexual perversions, incest, and sexual abuse of children.

Millions have abandoned biblical standards of conduct and are bartering the sacred experiences of marriage and parenthood for the bitter, remorseful fruits of sin. Not only are these evils damaging the familial structure of society, but the breakdown of the family in turn fosters and breeds these and other evils. The results in distorted lives of children and youth are distressing. The effects on society are both disastrous and cumulative.

These evils have become more open and threatening to the ideals and purposes of the Christian home. Adultery, pornography, abuse of any kind (including sexual abuse of spouses, children, and the elderly), incest, and homosexual and lesbian practices are among the perversions of God's original plan and illustrate the brokenness of humanity. As the intent of clear passages of Scripture (see Ex. 20:14; Lev. 18:22, 29; 20:13; 1 Cor. 6:9; 1 Tim. 1:10; Rom. 1:20-32) is denied and as their warnings are rejected in exchange for human opinions, much uncertainty and confusion prevail. Since ancient times and civilizations Satan's plan always has been to cause people to forget that God is their Creator and that when He created humankind in His own image, He created both "male and female" (Gen. 1:27).

Though God's Word alerts us to the degrading results of the world's obsession with sex and the pursuit of sensual pleasure, Christ came to destroy the works of Satan and reestablish the relationship of humans with their Creator. Though fallen in Adam and captive to sin, when we are in Christ we receive full pardon and the right to choose anew the better way to complete renewal. By means of the cross and the power of the Holy Spirit, we all may be freed from the grip of sinful practices as we are restored to the image of our Creator.

As parents and spiritual guides of youth, we must gain a sympathetic understanding of their problems, seek to provide for them a Christian social environment, and spiritually draw near to them so we can impart the ideals, inspiration, and power of Christianity.

Whatever may be the mistakes of our parents or peers, it is our responsibility and privilege to know and to hold the highest ideals of Christian manhood and womanhood. We can build Christian character that will buttress us against evil and make us uplifting influences in society by reverent Bible study, a deep acquaintance with the works of nature, rigorous guarding of the sacred powers of the body, earnest purpose, constancy in prayer, and sincere, unselfish ministry to others.

Social gatherings for both young and old should be occasions for happy fellowship and improvement of the powers of mind and soul, not for light and trifling amusement. Good music, elevating conversation, good recitations, suitable still or motion pictures, games carefully selected for educational value, and, above all, the making and using of plans for outreach (missionary) effort will bless and strengthen the lives of all. The Youth Ministries Department of the General Conference has published helpful information and practical suggestions for the conduct of social gatherings and for guidance in other social relations.

Our homes are by far the best places for social gatherings. In large centers where it is impossible to hold such gatherings in homes and where there is no social center of our own, we should secure a place free from influences destructive of Christian standards, rather than a place ordinarily used for commercial amusements and sports, such as social halls and skating rinks, which can suggest an atmosphere contrary to Christian standards.

Chaperonage

Chaperonage, the happy and cordial association of those older in years with young people, is one of the most wholesome influences in the lives of children and youth. "There is danger that both parents and teachers . . . fail to come sufficiently into social relation with their children or scholars."—CT 76. It is the duty of our homes, schools, and other institutions to care for the morals and reputation of those placed in our charge. As parents we should strongly support the regulations of the institutions serving our youth and children, and we should institute equal safeguards in our homes. To make this possible, we must learn how to be welcome companions of our children. But it rests chiefly upon the young people themselves to make chaperonage an honored and happy relationship.

Courtship

Courtship is recognized as a preparatory period during which a man and a woman, already mutually attracted, become more thoroughly acquainted with each other in preparation for intended marriage.

"Let those who are contemplating marriage weigh every sentiment and watch every development of character in the one with whom they think to unite their life destiny. Let every step toward a marriage alliance be characterized by modesty, simplicity, sincerity, and an earnest purpose to please and honor God. Marriage affects the afterlife both in this world and in the world to come. A sincere Christian will make no plans that God cannot approve."—MH 359.

Failure to follow these principles in Christian courtship may lead to tragedy. Unity of husband and wife in ideals and purposes is a requisite to a happy and successful home. Differences of partners regarding religion are likely to mar the happiness of the home and lead to confusion, perplexity, and failure in child rearing. The Bible advises, "Do not be unequally yoked together with unbelievers" (2 Cor. 6:14).

"The family tie is the closest, the most tender and sacred, of any on earth. It was designed to be a blessing to mankind. And it is a blessing wherever the marriage covenant is entered into intelligently, in the fear of God, and with due consideration for its responsibilities."—AH 18.

Worship of God, Sabbathkeeping, recreation, association, use of financial resources, and training of children are components of happy family relationships. Because differences in these areas can often lead to a deterioration of these relationships, to discouragement, and even to complete loss of Christian experience, an adequate preparation for marriage should include premarital pastoral counseling in these areas.

" 'Can two walk together, except they be agreed?' Amos 3:3. The happiness and prosperity of the marriage relation depends upon the unity of the parties; but between the believer and the unbeliever there is a radical difference of tastes, inclinations, and purposes. They are serving two masters, between whom there can be no concord. However pure and correct one's principles may be, the influence of an unbelieving companion will have a tendency to lead away from God."—PP 174.

The Spirit of Prophecy consistently counsels against marriage between "the believer and the unbeliever" and further cautions against uniting with fellow Christians who have "not accepted the truth for this time."—5T 364. Marriages are more likely to endure, and family life to fulfill the divine plan, if husband and wife are united and are bound together by common spiritual values and lifestyles. For these reasons the Church strongly discourages marriage between a Seventh-day Adventist and a member of another religion and strongly urges its pastors not to perform such marriages.

The Church recognizes that it is the prerogative of each individual member to make the final decision relative to the choice of a marriage partner. However, it is the hope of the Church that if the member chooses a partner who is not a member of the Church, the couple will realize and appreciate that the Seventh-day Adventist pastor, who has covenanted to uphold the principles outlined above, should not be expected to perform the marriage.

If a member does enter into such a marriage, the church is to demonstrate love and concern with the purpose of encouraging the couple toward complete unity in Christ.

Marriage

Marriage is a divine institution established by God Himself before the Fall, when everything, including marriage, was "very good" (Gen. 1:31). "Therefore a man shall leave his father and mother and be joined to his wife, and they shall become one flesh" (Gen. 2:24). "God celebrated the first marriage. Thus the institution has for its originator the Creator of the universe. 'Marriage is honourable'; it was one of the first gifts of God to man, and it is one of the two institutions that, after the fall, Adam brought with him beyond the gates of Paradise."—AH 25, 26.

God intended the marriage of Adam and Eve to be the pattern for all future marriages, and Christ endorsed this original concept: "Have you not read that He who made them at the beginning 'made them male and female,' and said, 'For this reason a man shall leave his father and mother and be joined to his wife, and the two shall become one flesh'? So then, they are no longer two but one flesh. Therefore what God has joined together, let not man separate" (Matt. 19:4-6). Marriage, thus instituted by God, is a monogamous, heterosexual relationship between one male and one female.

As such, marriage is a public, lawfully binding lifelong commitment of a man and a woman to each other and between the couple and God (Mark 10:2-9; Rom. 7:2). Paul indicates that the commitment that Christ has for the church is a model of the relationship between husband and wife (Eph. 5:31, 32). God intended marriage to be as permanent as Christ's relationship with the church.

Sexual intimacy within marriage is a sacred gift from God to the human family. It is an integral part of marriage, reserved for marriage only (Gen. 2:24; Prov. 5:5-20). Such intimacy, designed to be shared exclusively between husband and wife, promotes ever-increasing closeness, happiness, and security, and provides for the perpetuation of the human race.

Unity in marriage is achieved by mutual respect and love. No one is superior (Eph. 5:21-28). "Marriage, a union for life, is a symbol of the union between Christ and His church. The spirit that Christ manifests toward the church is the spirit that husband and wife are to manifest toward each other."—7T 46. God's Word condemns violence in personal relationships (Gen. 6:11, 13; Ps. 11:5; Isa. 58:4, 5; Rom. 13:10; Gal. 5:19-21). It is the spirit of Christ to love and accept, to seek to affirm and build others up, rather than to abuse or demean them (Rom. 12:10; 14:19; Eph. 4:26; 5:28, 29; Col. 3:8-14; 1 Thess. 5:11). There is no room among Christ's followers for tyrannical control and the abuse of power (Matt. 20:25-28; Eph. 6:4). Violence in the setting of marriage and family is abhorrent (see AH 343).

"Neither husband nor wife is to make a plea for rulership. The Lord has laid down the principle that is to guide in this matter. The husband is to cherish his wife as Christ cherishes the church. And the wife is to respect and love her husband. Both are to cultivate the spirit of kindness, being determined never to grieve or injure the other."—7T 47.

The entrance of sin adversely affected marriage. When Adam and Eve sinned, they lost the oneness that they had known with God and with each other (Gen. 3:6-24). Their relationship became marked with guilt, shame, blame, and pain. Wherever sin reigns, its sad effects on marriage include alienation, unfaithfulness, neglect, abuse, sexual perversion, domination of one partner by the other, violence, separation, desertion, and divorce.

Marriages involving more than one husband and one wife are also an expression of the effects of sin on the institution of marriage. Such marriages, though practiced in Old Testament times, are not in harmony with the divine design. God's plan for marriage requires His people to transcend the mores of popular culture that conflict with the biblical view.

The Christian concept of marriage includes the following:

1. *Divine Ideal to Be Restored in Christ*—In redeeming the world from sin and its consequences, God seeks to restore marriage to its original ideal. This is envisioned for the lives of those who have been born again into Christ's kingdom, those whose hearts are being sanctified by the Holy Spirit and who have as their primary purpose the exaltation of the Lord Jesus Christ. (See also 1 Peter 3:7; TMB 64.)

2. *Oneness and Equality to Be Restored in Christ*—The gospel emphasizes the love and submission of husband and wife to one another (1 Cor. 7:3, 4; Eph. 5:21). The model for the husband's leadership is the self-sacrificial love and service that Christ gives to the Church (Eph. 5:24, 25). Both Peter and Paul speak about the need for respect in the marriage relationship (1 Peter 3:7; Eph. 5:22, 23).

3. *Grace Available for All*—God seeks to restore to wholeness and reconcile to Himself all who have failed to attain the divine standard (2 Cor. 5:19). This includes those who have experienced broken marriage relationships.

4. *Role of the Church*—Moses in the Old Testament and Paul in the New Testament dealt with the problems caused by broken marriages (Deut. 24:1-5; 1 Cor. 7:11). Both, while upholding and affirming the ideal, worked constructively and redemptively with those who had fallen short of the divine standard. Similarly, the Church today is called to uphold and affirm God's ideal for marriage and, at the same time, to be a forgiving, reconciling, healing community, showing understanding and compassion when brokenness occurs.

Divorce

Divorce is contrary to God's original purpose in creating marriage (Matt. 19:3-8; Mark 10:2-9), but the Bible is not silent about it. Because divorce occurred as part of the fallen human experience, biblical legislation was given to limit the damage it caused (Deut. 24:1-4). The Bible consistently seeks to elevate marriage and to discourage divorce by describing the joys of married love and faithfulness (Prov. 5:18-20; Song of Sol. 2:16; 4:9-5:1), by referring to the marriage-like relationship of God with His people (Isa. 54:5; Jer. 3:1), by focusing on the possibilities of forgiveness and marital renewal (Hosea 3:1-3), and by indicating God's abhorrence of divorce and the misery it causes (Mal. 2:15, 16). Jesus restored the creation view of marriage as a lifelong commitment between a man and a woman and between the couple and God (Matt. 19:4-6; Mark 10:6-9). Much biblical instruction affirms marriage and seeks to correct problems that tend to weaken or destroy the foundation of marriage (Eph. 5:21-33; Heb. 13:4; 1 Peter 3:7).

Marriage rests on principles of love, loyalty, exclusiveness, trust, and support upheld by both partners in obedience to God (Gen. 2:24; Matt. 19:6; 1 Cor. 13; Eph. 5:21-29; 1 Thess. 4:1-7). When these principles are violated, Scripture acknowledges that tragic circumstances can destroy marriage.

Divine grace is the only remedy for the brokenness of divorce. When marriage fails, former partners should be encouraged to examine their experience and to seek God's will for their lives. God provides comfort to those who have been wounded. God also accepts the repentance of individuals who commit the most destructive sins, even those that carry with them irreparable consequences (2 Sam. 11; 12; Ps. 34:18; 86:5; Joel 2:12, 13; John 8:2-11; 1 John 1:9).

Scripture recognizes adultery and fornication (Matt. 5:32) and abandonment by an unbelieving partner (1 Cor. 7:10-15) as grounds for divorce.

There is no direct teaching in Scripture regarding remarriage after divorce. However, there is a strong implication in Jesus' words in Matthew 19:9 that would allow the remarriage of one who has remained faithful but whose spouse has been unfaithful to the marriage vow.

Church's Position on Divorce and Remarriage

Acknowledging the biblical teachings on marriage, the Church is aware that marriage relationships are less than ideal in many cases. The problem of divorce and remarriage can be seen in its true light only as it is viewed from Heaven's viewpoint and against the background of the Garden of Eden.

Central to God's holy plan for our world was the creation of beings made in His image who would multiply and replenish the earth and live together in purity, harmony, and happiness. He brought forth Eve from the side of Adam and gave her to Adam as his wife. Thus was marriage instituted—God the author of the institution and the officiator at the first marriage. After the Lord had revealed to Adam that Eve was verily bone of his bone and flesh of his flesh, there could never arise a doubt in his mind that the two of them were one flesh. Nor could ever a doubt arise in the mind of either of the holy pair that God intended that their home should endure forever.

The Church adheres to this view of marriage and the home without reservation, believing that any lowering of this high view is to that extent a lowering of the heavenly ideal. The belief that marriage is a divine institution rests upon the Holy Scriptures. Accordingly, all thinking and reasoning in the perplexing field of divorce and remarriage must constantly be harmonized with that holy ideal revealed in Eden.

The Church believes in the law of God and also in the forgiving mercy of God. It believes that victory and salvation can as surely be found by those who have transgressed in the matter of divorce and remarriage as by those who have failed in any other of God's holy standards.

Nothing presented here is intended to minimize the mercy of God or the forgiveness of God. In the fear of the Lord, the Church here sets forth the principles and practices that should apply in this matter of marriage, divorce, and remarriage.

Though marriage was first performed by God alone, it is recognized that people now live under civil governments; therefore, marriage has both divine and civil aspects. The divine aspect is governed by the laws of God, the civil by the laws of the state.

In harmony with these teachings, the following statements set forth the position of the Church:

1. When Jesus said, "Let not man put asunder," He established a rule of conduct for the Church, under the dispensation of grace, that must transcend all civil enactments that would go beyond His interpretation of the divine law governing the marriage relation. Here He gives a rule to which His followers should adhere even if the state or prevailing custom allows larger liberty. "In the Sermon on the Mount Jesus declared plainly that there could be no dissolution of the marriage tie, except for unfaithfulness to the marriage vow."—TMB 63. (Also see Matt. 5:32; 19:9.)

2. Unfaithfulness to the marriage vow has generally been seen to mean adultery or fornication. However, the New Testament word for fornication includes certain other sexual irregularities (1 Cor. 6:9; 1

Tim. 1:9, 10; Rom. 1:24-27). Therefore, sexual perversions, including incest, child sexual abuse, and homosexual practices, are also recognized as a misuse of sexual powers and a violation of the divine intention in marriage. As such they are just cause for separation or divorce.

Even though the Scriptures allow divorce for the reasons mentioned above, as well as for abandonment by an unbelieving spouse (1 Cor. 7:10-15), the church and those concerned should make earnest endeavors to effect a reconciliation, urging the spouses to manifest toward each other a Christlike spirit of forgiveness and restoration. The church is urged to relate lovingly and redemptively toward the couple in order to assist in the reconciliation process.

3.   In the event that reconciliation is not effected, the spouse who has remained faithful to the spouse who violated the marriage vow has the biblical right to secure a divorce and also to remarry.

4.   A spouse who has violated the marriage vow (see sections 1 and 2 above) shall be subject to discipline by the local church. (See pp. 62-68.) If genuinely repentant, the spouse may be placed under censure for a stated period of time rather than removed from church membership. A spouse who gives no evidence of full and sincere repentance shall be removed from membership. In case the violation has brought public reproach on the cause of God, the church, in order to maintain its high standards and good name, may remove the individual from membership.

Any of these forms of discipline shall be applied by the church in a manner that would seek to attain the two objectives of discipline—to correct and redeem. In the gospel of Christ, the redemptive side of discipline is always tied to an authentic transformation of the sinner into a new creature in Jesus Christ.

5.   A spouse who has violated the marriage vow and who is divorced does not have the moral right to marry another while the spouse who has been faithful to the marriage vow still lives and remains unmarried and chaste. The person who does so shall be removed from membership. The person whom he/she marries, if a member, also shall be removed from membership.

6.   It is recognized that sometimes marriage relations deteriorate to the point where it is better for a husband and wife to separate. "Now to the married I command, yet not I but the Lord: A wife is not to depart from her husband. But even if she does depart, let her remain unmarried or be reconciled to her husband. And a husband is not to divorce his wife" (1 Cor. 7:10, 11). In many such cases, the custody of children, the adjustment of property rights, or even personal protection may necessitate a

change in marital status. In such cases it may be permissible in some countries to secure what is known as a legal separation. However, in some jurisdictions such a separation can be secured only by divorce.

A separation or divorce that results from factors such as physical violence or in which "unfaithfulness to the marriage vow" (see sections 1 and 2 above) is not involved does not give either one the scriptural right to remarry, unless in the meantime the other party has remarried, committed adultery or fornication, or died. Should a member who has been thus divorced remarry without these biblical grounds, he/she shall be removed from membership, and the one whom he/she marries, if a member, also shall be removed from membership. (See pp. 62-68.)

7. A spouse who has violated the marriage vow and has been divorced and removed from membership and who has remarried, or a person who has been divorced on other than the grounds set forth in sections 1 and 2 above and has remarried, and who has been removed from membership, shall be considered ineligible for membership except as provided below.

8. The marriage contract is not only sacred but also possibly more complex when, for example, it involves children. Hence, in a request for readmittance to membership, the options available to the repentant may be severely limited. Before final action is taken by the church, the request for readmittance shall be brought by the church through the pastor or district leader to the conference committee for counsel and recommendation of steps the repentant one, or ones, may take to secure readmittance.

9. Readmittance to membership of those who have been removed for reasons given in the foregoing sections shall normally be on the basis of rebaptism. (See pp. 49, 67, 68.)

10. When a person who has been removed from membership is readmitted to membership, as provided in section 8, every care should be exercised to safeguard the unity and harmony of the church by not giving that person responsibility as a leader, especially in an office that requires the rite of ordination, unless by very careful counsel with conference administration.

11. No pastor has the right to officiate at the remarriage of any person who, under the stipulation of the preceding paragraphs, has no scriptural right to remarry.

Local Church Ministry for Families

The Church as a redemptive agency of Christ is to minister to its members in all of their needs and to nurture everyone so that all may grow into a mature Christian experience. This is particularly true when members face lifelong decisions such as marriage and distressful experiences such as divorce. When a couple's marriage is in danger of breaking down, every effort should be made by the partners and those in the church or family who minister to them to bring about their reconciliation in harmony with divine principles for restoring wounded relationships (Hosea 3:1-3; 1 Cor. 7:10, 11; 13:4-7; Gal. 6:1).

Resources that can be of assistance to members in the development of a strong Christian home are available through the church or other church organizations. These resources include: (1) programs of orientation for couples engaged to be married, (2) programs of instruction for married couples with their families, and (3) programs of support for broken families and divorced individuals.

Pastoral support is vital in the area of instruction and orientation in the case of marriage, and healing and restoration in the case of divorce. The pastoral function in the latter case is both disciplinary and supportive. That function includes the sharing of relevant information, some of which may be sensitive and must be handled with great discretion. However, this ethical concern alone should not be the grounds for avoiding disciplinary actions established in sections 1-11 above.

Just as God forgives, members are called to forgive and to accept those who have failed (Isa. 54:5-8; Matt. 6:14, 15; Eph. 4:32). The Bible urges patience, compassion, and forgiveness in the Christian care of those who have erred (Matt. 18:10-20; Gal. 6:1, 2). While individuals are under discipline, either by censure or by being removed from membership, the church, as an instrument of God's mission, shall make every effort to maintain caring and spiritually nurturing contact with them.

CHAPTER 14

Fundamental Beliefs of Seventh-day Adventists

Seventh-day Adventists accept the Bible as their only creed and hold certain fundamental beliefs to be the teaching of the Holy Scriptures. These beliefs, as set forth here, constitute the church's understanding and expression of the teaching of Scripture. Revision of these statements may be expected at a General Conference Session when the church is led by the Holy Spirit to a fuller understanding of Bible truth or finds better language in which to express the teachings of God's Holy Word.

1. *The Holy Scriptures*

The Holy Scriptures, Old and New Testaments, are the written Word of God, given by divine inspiration. The inspired authors spoke and wrote as they were moved by the Holy Spirit. In this Word, God has committed to humanity the knowledge necessary for salvation. The Holy Scriptures are the supreme, authoritative, and the infallible revelation of His will. They are the standard of character, the test of experience, the definitive revealer of doctrines, and the trustworthy record of God's acts in history. (Ps. 119:105; Prov 30:5, 6; Isa. 8:20; John 17:17; 1 Thess. 2:13; 2 Tim. 3:16, 17; Heb. 4:12; 2 Peter 1:20, 21.)

2. *The Trinity*

There is one God: Father, Son, and Holy Spirit, a unity of three coeternal Persons. God is immortal, all-powerful, all-knowing, above all, and ever present. He is infinite and beyond human comprehension, yet known through His self-revelation. God, who is love, is forever worthy of worship, adoration, and service by the whole creation. (Gen. 1:26; Deut. 6:4; Isa. 6:8; Matt. 28:19; John 3:16; 2 Cor. 1:21, 22; 13:14; Eph. 4:4-6; 1 Peter 1:2.)

3. *The Father*

God the eternal Father is the Creator, Source, Sustainer, and Sovereign of all creation. He is just and holy, merciful and gracious, slow to anger, and abounding in steadfast love and faithfulness. The qualities and powers exhibited in the Son and the Holy Spirit are also those of the Father. (Gen. 1:1; Deut. 4:35; Ps. 110:1, 4; John 3:16; 14:9; 1 Cor. 15:28; 1 Tim. 1:17; 1 John 4:8; Rev. 4:11.)

4.   *The Son*

God the eternal Son became incarnate in Jesus Christ. Through Him all things were created, the character of God is revealed, the salvation of humanity is accomplished, and the world is judged. Forever truly God, He became also truly human, Jesus the Christ. He was conceived of the Holy Spirit and born of the virgin Mary. He lived and experienced temptation as a human being, but perfectly exemplified the righteousness and love of God. By His miracles He manifested God's power and was attested as God's promised Messiah. He suffered and died voluntarily on the cross for our sins and in our place, was raised from the dead, and ascended to heaven to minister in the heavenly sanctuary in our behalf. He will come again in glory for the final deliverance of His people and the restoration of all things. (Isa. 53:4-6; Dan. 9:25-27; Luke 1:35; John 1:1-3, 14; 5:22; 10:30; 14:1-3, 9, 13; Rom. 6:23; 1 Cor. 15:3, 4; 2 Cor. 3:18; 5:17-19; Phil. 2:5-11; Col. 1:15-19; Heb. 2:9-18; 8:1, 2.)

5.   *The Holy Spirit*

God the eternal Spirit was active with the Father and the Son in Creation, incarnation, and redemption. He is as much a person as are the Father and the Son. He inspired the writers of Scripture. He filled Christ's life with power. He draws and convicts human beings; and those who respond He renews and transforms into the image of God. Sent by the Father and the Son to be always with His children, He extends spiritual gifts to the church, empowers it to bear witness to Christ, and in harmony with the Scriptures leads it into all truth. (Gen. 1:1, 2; 2 Sam. 23:2; Ps. 51:11; Isa. 61:1; Luke 1:35; 4:18; John 14:16-18, 26; 15:26; 16:7-13; Acts 1:8; 5:3; 10:38; Rom. 5:5; 1 Cor. 12:7-11; 2 Cor. 3:18; 2 Peter 1:21.)

6.   *Creation*

God has revealed in Scripture the authentic and historical account of His creative activity. He created the universe, and in a recent six-day creation the Lord made "the heavens and the earth, the sea, and all that is in them" and rested on the seventh day. Thus He established the Sabbath as a perpetual memorial of the work He performed and completed during six literal days that together with the Sabbath constituted the same unit of time that we call a week today. The first man and woman were made in the image of God as the crowning work of Creation, given dominion over the world, and charged with responsibility to care for it. When the world was finished it was "very good," declaring the glory of God. (Gen. 1-2; 5; 11;

Ex. 20:8-11; Ps. 19:1-6; 33:6, 9; 104; Isa. 45:12, 18; Acts 17:24; Col. 1:16; Heb. 1:2; 11:3; Rev. 10:6; 14:7.)

7. *The Nature of Humanity*

Man and woman were made in the image of God with individuality, the power and freedom to think and to do. Though created free beings, each is an indivisible unity of body, mind, and spirit, dependent upon God for life and breath and all else. When our first parents disobeyed God, they denied their dependence upon Him and fell from their high position. The image of God in them was marred and they became subject to death. Their descendants share this fallen nature and its consequences. They are born with weaknesses and tendencies to evil. But God in Christ reconciled the world to Himself and by His Spirit restores in penitent mortals the image of their Maker. Created for the glory of God, they are called to love Him and one another, and to care for their environment. (Gen. 1:26-28; 2:7, 15; 3; Ps. 8:4-8; 51:5, 10; 58:3; Jer. 17:9; Acts 17:24-28; Rom. 5:12-17; 2 Cor. 5:19, 20; Eph. 2:3; 1 Thess. 5:23; 1 John 3:4; 4:7, 8, 11, 20.)

8. *The Great Controversy*

All humanity is now involved in a great controversy between Christ and Satan regarding the character of God, His law, and His sovereignty over the universe. This conflict originated in heaven when a created being, endowed with freedom of choice, in self-exaltation became Satan, God's adversary, and led into rebellion a portion of the angels. He introduced the spirit of rebellion into this world when he led Adam and Eve into sin. This human sin resulted in the distortion of the image of God in humanity, the disordering of the created world, and its eventual devastation at the time of the global flood, as presented in the historical account of Genesis 1-11. Observed by the whole creation, this world became the arena of the universal conflict, out of which the God of love will ultimately be vindicated. To assist His people in this controversy, Christ sends the Holy Spirit and the loyal angels to guide, protect, and sustain them in the way of salvation. (Gen. 3; 6-8; Job 1:6-12; Isa. 14:12-14; Ezek. 28:12-18; Rom. 1:19-32; 3:4; 5:12-21; 8:19-22; 1 Cor. 4:9; Heb. 1:14; 1 Peter 5:8; 2 Peter 3:6; Rev. 12:4-9.)

9. *The Life, Death, and Resurrection of Christ*

In Christ's life of perfect obedience to God's will, His suffering, death, and resurrection, God provided the only means of atonement for human sin, so that those who by faith accept this atonement may have eternal life, and the whole creation may better understand the infinite and holy love of the Creator. This perfect atonement vindicates the righteousness of God's law and the graciousness of His character; for it both condemns our sin and provides for our forgiveness. The death of Christ is substitutionary and expiatory, reconciling and transforming. The bodily resurrection of Christ proclaims God's triumph over the forces of evil, and for those who accept the atonement assures their final victory over sin and death. It declares the Lordship of Jesus Christ, before whom every knee in heaven and on earth will bow. (Gen. 3:15; Ps. 22:1; Isa. 53; John 3:16; 14:30; Rom. 1:4; 3:25; 4:25; 8:3, 4; 1 Cor. 15:3, 4, 20-22; 2 Cor. 5:14, 15, 19-21; Phil. 2:6-11; Col. 2:15; 1 Peter 2:21, 22; 1 John 2:2; 4:10.)

10. *The Experience of Salvation*

In infinite love and mercy God made Christ, who knew no sin, to be sin for us, so that in Him we might be made the righteousness of God. Led by the Holy Spirit we sense our need, acknowledge our sinfulness, repent of our transgressions, and exercise faith in Jesus as Saviour and Lord, Substitute and Example. This saving faith comes through the divine power of the Word and is the gift of God's grace. Through Christ we are justified, adopted as God's sons and daughters, and delivered from the lordship of sin. Through the Spirit we are born again and sanctified; the Spirit renews our minds, writes God's law of love in our hearts, and we are given the power to live a holy life. Abiding in Him we become partakers of the divine nature and have the assurance of salvation now and in the judgment. (Gen. 3:15; Isa. 45:22; 53; Jer. 31:31-34; Ezck. 33:11; 36:25-27; Hab. 2:4; Mark 9:23, 24; John 3:3-8, 16; 16:8; Rom. 3:21-26; 5:6-10; 8:1-4, 14-17; 10:17; 12:2; 2 Cor. 5:17-21; Gal. 1:4; 3:13, 14, 26; 4:4-7; Eph. 2:4-10; Col. 1:13, 14; Titus 3:3-7; Heb. 8:7-12; 1 Peter 1:23; 2:21, 22; 2 Peter 1:3, 4; Rev. 13:8.)

11. *Growing in Christ*

By His death on the cross Jesus triumphed over the forces of evil. He who subjugated the demonic spirits during His earthly ministry has broken their power and made certain their ultimate doom. Jesus' victory gives us victory over the evil forces that still seek to control us, as we walk with Him in peace, joy, and assurance of His love. Now the Holy Spirit dwells within us and empowers us. Continually committed to Jesus as our Saviour and Lord, we are set free from the burden of our past deeds. No longer do we live in the darkness, fear of evil powers, ignorance, and meaninglessness of our former way of life. In this new freedom in Jesus, we are called to grow into the likeness of His character, communing with Him daily in prayer, feeding on His Word, meditating on it and on His providence, singing His praises, gathering together for worship, and participating in the mission of the Church. We are also called to follow Christ's example by compassionately ministering to the physical, mental, social, emotional, and spiritual needs of humanity. As we give ourselves in loving service to those around us and in witnessing to His salvation, His constant presence with us through the Spirit transforms every moment and every task into a spiritual experience. (1 Chron. 29:11; Ps. 1:1, 2; 23:4; 77:11, 12; Matt. 20:25-28; 25:31-46; Luke 10:17-20; John 20:21; Rom. 8:38, 39; 2 Cor. 3:17, 18; Gal. 5:22-25; Eph. 5:19, 20; 6:12-18; Phil. 3:7-14; Col. 1:13, 14; 2:6, 14, 15; 1 Thess. 5:16-18, 23; Heb. 10:25; James 1:27; 2 Peter 2:9; 3:18; 1 John 4:4.)

12. *The Church*

The church is the community of believers who confess Jesus Christ as Lord and Saviour. In continuity with the people of God in Old Testament times, we are called out from the world; and we join together for worship, for fellowship, for instruction in the Word, for the celebration of the Lord's Supper, for service to humanity, and for the worldwide proclamation of the gospel. The church derives its authority from Christ, who is the incarnate Word revealed in the Scriptures. The church is God's family; adopted by Him as children, its members live on the basis of the new covenant. The church is the body of Christ, a community of faith of which Christ Himself is the Head. The church is the bride for whom Christ died that He might sanctify and cleanse her. At His return in triumph, He will present her to Himself a glorious church, the faithful of all the ages, the purchase of His blood, not having spot or wrinkle, but holy and without blemish. (Gen. 12:1-3; Exod. 19:3-7; Matt. 16:13-20; 18:18; 28:19, 20; Acts 2:38-42; 7:38; 1 Cor. 1:2; Eph. 1:22, 23; 2:19-22; 3:8-11; 5:23-27; Col. 1:17, 18; 1 Peter 2:9.)

13. *The Remnant and Its Mission*

The universal church is composed of all who truly believe in Christ, but in the last days, a time of widespread apostasy, a remnant has been called out to keep the commandments of God and the faith of Jesus. This remnant announces the arrival of the judgment hour, proclaims salvation through Christ, and heralds the approach of His second advent. This proclamation is symbolized by the three angels of Revelation 14; it coincides with the work of judgment in heaven and results in a work of repentance and reform on earth. Every believer is called to have a personal part in this worldwide witness. (Dan. 7:9-14; Isa. 1:9; 11:11; Jer. 23:3; Mic. 2:12; 2 Cor. 5:10; 1 Peter 1:16-19; 4:17; 2 Peter 3:10-14; Jude 3, 14; Rev. 12:17; 14:6-12; 18:1-4.)

14. *Unity in the Body of Christ*

The church is one body with many members, called from every nation, kindred, tongue, and people. In Christ we are a new creation; distinctions of race, culture, learning, and nationality, and differences between high and low, rich and poor, male and female, must not be divisive among us. We are all equal in Christ, who by one Spirit has bonded us into one fellowship with Him and with one another; we are to serve and be served without partiality or reservation. Through the revelation of Jesus Christ in the Scriptures we share the same faith and hope, and reach out in one witness to all. This unity has its source in the oneness of the triune God, who has adopted us as His children. (Ps. 133:1; Matt. 28:19, 20; John 17:20-23; Acts 17:26, 27; Rom. 12:4, 5; 1 Cor. 12:12-14; 2 Cor. 5:16, 17; Gal. 3:27-29; Eph. 2:13-16; 4:3-6, 11-16; Col. 3:10-15.)

15. *Baptism*

By baptism we confess our faith in the death and resurrection of Jesus Christ, and testify of our death to sin and of our purpose to walk in newness of life. Thus we acknowledge Christ as Lord and Saviour, become His people, and are received as members by His church. Baptism is a symbol of our union with Christ, the forgiveness of our sins, and our reception of the Holy Spirit. It is by immersion in water and is contingent on an affirmation of faith in Jesus and evidence of repentance of sin. It follows instruction in the Holy Scriptures and acceptance of their teachings. (Matt. 28:19, 20; Acts 2:38; 16:30-33; 22:16; Rom. 6:1-6; Gal. 3:27; Col. 2:12, 13.)

16. *The Lord's Supper*

The Lord's Supper is a participation in the emblems of the body and blood of Jesus as an expression of faith in Him, our Lord and Saviour. In this experience of communion Christ is present to meet and strengthen His people. As we partake, we joyfully proclaim the Lord's death until He comes again. Preparation for the Supper includes self-examination, repentance, and confession. The Master ordained the service of foot-washing to signify renewed cleansing, to express a willingness to serve one another in Christlike humility, and to unite our hearts in love. The communion service is open to all believing Christians. (Matt. 26:17-30; John 6:48-63; 13:1-17; 1 Cor. 10:16, 17; 11:23-30; Rev. 3:20.)

17. *Spiritual Gifts and Ministries*

God bestows upon all members of His church in every age spiritual gifts that each member is to employ in loving ministry for the common good of the church and of humanity. Given by the agency of the Holy Spirit, who apportions to each member as He wills, the gifts provide all abilities and ministries needed by the church to fulfill its divinely ordained functions. According to the Scriptures, these gifts include such ministries as faith, healing, prophecy, proclamation, teaching, administration, reconciliation, compassion, and self-sacrificing service and charity for the help and encouragement of people. Some members are called of God and endowed by the Spirit for functions recognized by the church in pastoral, evangelistic, and teaching ministries particularly needed to equip the members for service, to build up the church to spiritual maturity, and to foster unity of the faith and knowledge of God. When members employ these spiritual gifts as faithful stewards of God's varied grace, the church is protected from the destructive influence of false doctrine, grows with a growth that is from God, and is built up in faith and love. (Acts 6:1-7; Rom. 12:4-8; 1 Cor. 12:7-11, 27, 28; Eph. 4:8, 11-16; 1 Tim. 3:1-13; 1 Peter 4:10, 11.)

18. *The Gift of Prophecy*

The Scriptures testify that one of the gifts of the Holy Spirit is prophecy. This gift is an identifying mark of the remnant church and we believe it was manifested in the ministry of Ellen G. White. Her writings speak with prophetic authority and provide comfort, guidance, instruction, and correction to the church. They also make clear that the Bible is the standard by which all teaching and experience must be tested. (Num. 12:6; 2 Chron. 20:20; Amos 3:7; Joel 2:28, 29; Acts 2:14-21; 2 Tim. 3:16, 17; Heb. 1:1-3; Rev. 12:17; 19:10; 22:8, 9.)

19. *The Law of God*

The great principles of God's law are embodied in the Ten Commandments and exemplified in the life of Christ. They express God's love, will, and purposes concerning human conduct and relationships and are binding upon all people in every age. These precepts are the basis of God's covenant with His people and the standard in God's judgment. Through the agency of the Holy Spirit they point out sin and awaken a sense of need for a Saviour. Salvation is all of grace and not of works, and its fruit is obedience to the Commandments. This obedience develops Christian character and results in a sense of well-being. It is ~~an~~ evidence of our love for the Lord and our concern for our fellow human beings. The obedience of faith demonstrates the power of Christ to transform lives, and therefore strengthens Christian witness. (Exod. 20:1-17; Deut. 28:1-14; Ps. 19:7-14; 40:7, 8; Matt. 5:17-20; 22:36-40; John 14:15; 15:7-10; Rom. 8:3, 4; Eph. 2:8-10; Heb. 8:8-10; 1 John 2:3; 5:3; Rev. 12:17; 14:12.)

20. *The Sabbath*

The gracious Creator, after the six days of Creation, rested on the seventh day and instituted the Sabbath for all people as a memorial of Creation. The fourth commandment of God's unchangeable law requires the observance of this seventh-day Sabbath as the day of rest, worship, and ministry in harmony with the teaching and practice of Jesus, the Lord of the Sabbath. The Sabbath is a day of delightful communion with God and one another. It is a symbol of our redemption in Christ, a sign of our sanctification, a token of our allegiance, and a foretaste of our eternal future in God's kingdom. The Sabbath is God's perpetual sign of His eternal covenant between Him and His people. Joyful observance of this holy time from evening to evening, sunset to sunset, is a celebration of God's creative and redemptive acts. (Gen. 2:1-3; Exod. 20:8-11; 31:13-17; Lev. 23:32; Deut. 5:12-15; Isa. 56:5, 6; 58:13, 14; Ezek. 20:12, 20; Matt. 12:1-12; Mark 1:32; Luke 4:16; Heb. 4:1-11.)

21. *Stewardship*

We are God's stewards, entrusted by Him with time and opportunities, abilities and possessions, and the blessings of the earth and its resources. We are responsible to Him for their proper use. We acknowledge God's ownership by faithful service to Him and our fellow human beings, and by returning tithe and giving offerings for the proclamation of His gospel and the support and growth of His church. Stewardship is a privilege given to us by God for nurture in love and the victory over selfishness and covetousness. Stewards rejoice in the blessings that come to others as a result of their faithfulness. (Gen. 1:26-28; 2:15; 1 Chron. 29:14; Haggai 1:3-11; Mal. 3:8-12; Matt. 23:23; Rom. 15:26, 27; 1 Cor. 9:9-14; 2 Cor. 8:1-15; 9:7.)

22. *Christian Behavior*

We are called to be a godly people who think, feel, and act in harmony with biblical principles in all aspects of personal and social life. For the Spirit to recreate in us the character of our Lord we involve ourselves only in those things that will produce Christlike purity, health, and joy in our lives. This means that our amusement and entertainment should meet the highest standards of Christian taste and beauty. While recognizing cultural differences, our dress is to be simple, modest, and neat, befitting those whose true beauty does not consist of outward adornment but in the imperishable ornament of a gentle and quiet spirit. It also means that because our bodies are the temples of the Holy Spirit, we are to care for them intelligently. Along with adequate exercise and rest, we are to adopt the most healthful diet possible and abstain from the unclean foods identified in the Scriptures. Since alcoholic beverages, tobacco, and the irresponsible use of drugs and narcotics are harmful to our bodies, we are to abstain from them as well. Instead, we are to engage in whatever brings our thoughts and bodies into the discipline of Christ, who desires our wholesomeness, joy, and goodness. (Gen. 7:2; Exod. 20:15; Lev. 11:1-47; Ps. 106:3; Rom. 12:1, 2; 1 Cor. 6:19, 20; 10:31; 2 Cor. 6:14-7:1; 10:5; Eph. 5:1-21; Phil. 2:4; 4:8; 1 Tim. 2:9, 10; Titus 2:11, 12; 1 Peter 3:1-4; 1 John 2:6; 3 John 2.)

23. *Marriage and the Family*

Marriage was divinely established in Eden and affirmed by Jesus to be a lifelong union between a man and a woman in loving companionship. For the Christian a marriage commitment is to God as well as to the spouse, and should be entered into only between a man and a woman who share a common faith. Mutual love, honor, respect, and responsibility are the fabric of this relationship, which is to reflect the love, sanctity, closeness, and permanence of the relationship between Christ and His church. Regarding divorce, Jesus taught that the person who divorces a spouse, except for fornication, and marries another, commits adultery. Although some family relationships may fall short of the ideal, a man and a woman who fully commit themselves to each other in Christ through marriage may achieve loving unity through the guidance of the Spirit and the nurture of the church. God blesses the family and intends that its members shall assist each other toward complete maturity. Increasing family closeness is one of the earmarks of the final gospel message. Parents are to bring up their children to love and obey the Lord. By their example and their words they are to teach them that Christ is a loving, tender, and caring guide who wants them to become members of His body, the family of God which embraces both single and married persons. (Gen. 2:18-25; Exod. 20:12; Deut. 6:5-9; Prov. 22:6; Mal. 4:5, 6; Matt. 5:31, 32; 19:3-9, 12; Mark 10:11, 12; John 2:1-11; 1 Cor. 7:7, 10, 11; 2 Cor. 6:14; Eph. 5:21-33; 6:1-4.)

24. *Christ's Ministry in the Heavenly Sanctuary*

There is a sanctuary in heaven, the true tabernacle that the Lord set up and not humans. In it Christ ministers on our behalf, making available to believers the benefits of His atoning sacrifice offered once for all on the cross. At His ascension, He was inaugurated as our great High Priest and, began His intercessory ministry, which was typified by the work of the high priest in the holy place of the earthly sanctuary. In 1844, at the end of the prophetic period of 2300 days, He entered the second and last phase of His atoning ministry, which was typified by the work of the high priest in the most holy place of the earthly sanctuary. It is a work of investigative judgment which is part of the ultimate disposition of all sin, typified by the cleansing of the ancient Hebrew sanctuary on the Day of Atonement. In that typical service the sanctuary was cleansed with the blood of animal sacrifices, but the heavenly things are purified with the perfect sacrifice of the blood of Jesus. The investigative judgment reveals to heavenly intelligences who among the dead are asleep in Christ and therefore, in Him, are deemed worthy to have part in the first resurrection. It also makes manifest who among the living are abiding in Christ, keeping the commandments of God and the faith of Jesus, and in Him, therefore, are ready for translation into His everlasting kingdom. This judgment vindicates the justice of God in saving those who believe in Jesus. It declares that those who have remained loyal to God shall receive the kingdom. The completion of this ministry of Christ will mark the close of human probation before the Second Advent. (Lev. 16; Num. 14:34; Ezek. 4:6; Dan. 7:9-27; 8:13, 14; 9:24-27; Heb. 1:3; 2:16, 17; 4:14-16; 8:1-5; 9:11-28; 10:19-22; Rev. 8:3-5; 11:19; 14:6, 7, 12; 20:12; 22:11, 12.)

25. *The Second Coming of Christ*

The second coming of Christ is the blessed hope of the church, the grand climax of the gospel. The Saviour's coming will be literal, personal, visible, and worldwide. When He returns, the righteous dead will be resurrected, and together with the righteous living will be glorified and taken to heaven, but the unrighteous will die. The almost complete fulfillment of most lines of prophecy, together with the present condition of the world, indicates that Christ's coming is near. The time of that event has not been revealed, and we are therefore exhorted to be ready at all times. (Matt. 24; Mark 13; Luke 21; John 14:1-3; Acts 1:9-11; 1 Cor. 15:51-54; 1 Thess. 4:13-18; 5:1-6; 2 Thess. 1:7-10; 2:8; 2 Tim. 3:1-5; Titus 2:13; Heb. 9:28; Rev. 1:7; 14:14-20; 19:11-21.)

26. *Death and Resurrection*

The wages of sin is death. But God, who alone is immortal, will grant eternal life to His redeemed. Until that day death is an unconscious state for all people. When Christ, who is our life, appears, the resurrected righteous and the living righteous will be glorified and caught up to meet their Lord. The second resurrection, the resurrection of the unrighteous, will take place a thousand years later. (Job 19:25-27; Ps. 146:3, 4; Eccl. 9:5, 6, 10; Dan. 12:2, 13; Isa. 25:8; John 5:28, 29; 11:11-14; Rom. 6:23; 1 Cor. 15:51-54; Col. 3:4; 1 Thess. 4:13-17; 1 Tim. 6:15, 16; Rev. 20:1-10.)

27. *The Millennium and the End of Sin*

The millennium is the thousand-year reign of Christ with His saints in heaven between the first and second resurrections. During this time the wicked dead will be judged; the earth will be utterly desolate, without living human inhabitants, but occupied by Satan and his angels. At its close Christ with His saints and the Holy City will descend from heaven to earth. The unrighteous dead will then be resurrected, and with Satan and his angels will surround the city; but fire from God will consume them and cleanse the earth. The universe will thus be freed of sin and sinners forever. (Jer. 4:23-26; Ezek. 28:18, 19; Mal. 4:1; 1 Cor. 6:2, 3; Rev. 20; 21:1-5.)

28. *The New Earth*

On the new earth, in which righteousness dwells, God will provide an eternal home for the redeemed and a perfect environment for everlasting life, love, joy, and learning in His presence. For here God Himself will dwell with His people, and suffering and death will have passed away. The great controversy will be ended, and sin will be no more. All things, animate and inanimate, will declare that God is love; and He shall reign forever. Amen. (Isa. 35; 65:17-25; Matt. 5:5; 2 Peter 3:13; Rev. 11:15; 21:1-7; 22:1-5.)

Notes

These notes contain explanatory material regarding how a church may proceed in a particular matter. A church may adopt alternative ways of handling such items. Such alternative methods should be in harmony with generally accepted principles of Church organization and operation.

CHAPTER 8 Notes

1.   *Marriage Ceremony* (see p. 75)—In some countries or states a pastor must be legally appointed and registered in order to conduct the marriage service. In many lands the pastor may perform the ceremony in the church, but the marriage contract is legally signed by the district registrar, who usually sits in the vestry and listens to the approved form of marriage declaration. In still other lands the pastor cannot perform the ceremony at all because it is recognized as a state responsibility and is looked upon as a civil contract. In such cases members usually retire to the home or place of worship, where a pastor conducts a special service to seek the blessing of the Lord upon the couple. (See pp. 153-160.)

2.   *Training and Equipping of Elders* (see p. 76)—While the pastor has the primary responsibility for training elders, conferences are encouraged to schedule periodic meetings for their training. In order to support a pastor-elder team relationship, pastors also should attend the training meetings. Leaders of companies who function in the place of elders also should be invited.

3.   *Training and Equipping of Deacons and Deaconesses* (see pp. 77 and 80)—While the pastor has the primary responsibility for the training of deacons and deaconesses, the Ministerial Association of the conference is encouraged to schedule periodic meetings for the training of the deacons and deaconesses.

4.   *Care and Maintenance of Church Property* (see pp. 79, 81)—Deacons and deaconesses must see that the church building is kept clean and in repair and that the grounds are kept clean and attractive. This also includes ensuring that janitorial work is done. In large churches where it is necessary to employ a janitor, the deacons should recommend a suitable person to the board, which votes to employ such help, or the board may authorize the deacons to employ a janitor. Board authorization should be

obtained for all major repair expenses. All bills for repairs, as well as for recurring expenses, such as water, electricity, and, fuel, are referred to the treasurer for payment.

5.   ***Clerk Keeps Records*** (see p. 81)—Board minutes should be recorded in the church record book, or in another appropriate record system adopted by the church, giving the time and date of meeting, number attending, and a report of all actions taken. The clerk should also make a list of committees appointed at the meeting, giving to the chairperson a list of the members of each committee, together with its terms of reference and an outline of work it is asked to do. The church record book may be secured from the Adventist Book Center or, in some countries, from the publishing house.

The church record book contains a place for recording membership, including columns showing how and when members are received or removed. This record must be kept chronologically, and supporting data for each entry also should be recorded in the section where minutes of membership actions are kept. The membership record must be accurately and currently maintained in order to show the official standing of the membership.

6.   ***Corresponding With Members*** (see p. 82)—The clerk should correspond frequently with absent members and should pass on to them news of church progress, encouraging them, in turn, to report their Christian activities each quarter.

7.   ***Money for Personal Literature Orders*** (see p. 84)—Where a local Adventist Book Center does not exist, members may place money for personal orders of literature, books, pamphlets, magazines, and subscriptions for periodicals in an envelope, with the order form properly filled out, and hand it to the personal ministries secretary. The treasurer then remits both order and payment for all such literature to the Adventist Book Center or to the publishing house, according to the system adopted by the conference. At the close of each quarter the personal ministries secretary will report to the church, at its quarterly business meeting, about the standing of its account with the Adventist Book Center and/or publishing house and shall provide a copy for the treasurer. (See p. 101.)

8.   ***Safeguarding Children***—Church should be a safe place to bring our children. Everyone involved with children who are minors must meet

all Church and legal standards and requirements. In order to safeguard our children, churches are encouraged to adopt policies that would provide a measure of safety and protection for children. Such policies should include the following:

 a. *Two-Adult Policy*—Have two adults present in children's classrooms or activities.

 b. *Open Door*—Discourage private or one-on-one contact and encourage an open-door policy in all situations. Where an open door is not possible, station a second adult at the door.

 c. *Volunteer Screening*—Have all volunteers complete a volunteer information form, check their references, and, if required by law, do a police background check.

 d. *Six-Month Policy*—Require a waiting period of six months for newly baptized or transferring members who have indicated a willingness to work with children.

 e. *Training*—Provide regular training for teachers and volunteers to help them understand and protect children and how to nurture their faith.

Local church leaders should consult with the conference in order to ascertain conference procedures and requirements, including local legal requirements for individuals working with children.

Additional resources are available from Adventist Risk Management at www.adventistrisk.org.

 9. **Children's Ministries Resources** (see p. 87)—*The Children's Ministries Handbook: A Step-by-Step Guide for Children's Leaders Around the World* (2005); *The Children's Ministries Coordinator: A Step-by-Step Guide for Organizing Children's Ministries in the Local Church* (2005); and *Pastor's and Elder's Handbook for Children's Ministries* (2005). Silver Spring, Md.: Children's Ministries, General Conference of Seventh-day Adventists. For further information, contact your local conference children's ministries director and www.gcchildmin.org.

 10. **Family Ministries Resources** (see p. 92)—*Caring for Families Today: A Guide for Family Ministries* (2009). Silver Spring, Md.: Family Ministries, General Conference of Seventh-day Adventists. For further information, contact your local conference family ministries director and www.adventist-familyministries.org.

 11. **Health Ministries Resources** (see p. 93)—*CELEBRATIONS* (a 12-program outline of the essential health ministry presentations,

includes scripts and PowerPoints), *CHARTERS* (a series of lectures with PowerPoint for presentation to lay audiences), *Foundations for Health Ministry* (84 lectures on basic health for health ministry leaders), *Breathe Free* (stop-smoking curriculum), Youth Alive (a program to build resiliency in our youth), *Vegetarian Cuisine Instructor's Course* (a comprehensive how-to manual), *Birthing Companions* (to support young pregnant women in their pregnancy), *Regeneration* (a 12-step program for recovery in addiction), and *My Vegetarian Food Pyramid* (posters large or small).

12. ***Public Affairs and Religious Liberty Resources*** (see p. 95)— For further information, contact your local conference Public Affairs and Religious Liberty director or visit www.parl.org and www.irla.org.

13. ***Publishing Ministries Resources*** (see p. 96)—*Literature Ministry Training Manual* (volumes 1-3 with PowerPoint presentations); *The Publishing Ministry and the Church* (booklet); *Student Literature Evangelism Manual*; *Miracles of Grace* (a book of 365 testimonies of literature evangelists around the world); *The Literature Evangelist* (a quarterly magazine of General Conference Publishing Ministries). For more information, contact your local conference or union publishing director. You can also go to publishing.gc.adventist.org.

14. ***Sabbath School and Personal Ministries Resources*** (see pp. 97, 100)—Sabbath School Bible study guides for various ages (*CQ*, *Cornerstone Connections*, *Real-Time Faith*, *PowerPoints*, *Primary*, *Kindergarten*, and *Beginner*); *In Step with Jesus* (a four-quarter Sabbath School Bible study guide for new members); *Sabbath School Handbook*; *Personal Ministries Handbook*; *Keys for Sabbath School and Personal Ministries Leaders* (a series of leaflets); *Reaching and Winning* (a series of booklets for personal ministries to peoples of various faith systems and other target groups); *Keys to Adventist Community Services* (a leaflet/handbook); *The Sharing* (departmental newsletter); and *Community Services and Urban Ministry Certification Program* (www.sabbathschoolpersonalministries.org/acs_iicm). For further information, contact the local conference Sabbath School and personal ministries director. Other resources may be found at www.sabbathschoolpersonalministries.org, GraceLink.net, JuniorPowerPoints.org, RealTimeFaith.net, CornerstoneConnections.net, CQBibleStudy.org, SabbathSchoolU.org, InStepWithJesus.org, or the Sabbath School app can be downloaded on a mobile device.

15. ***Adventist Community Services*** (see pp. 101 and 102)—Some territories continue to have an active Dorcas Society and Adventist Men, or have alternate names for social ministry out of the local church that have been officially approved by regional church administrative units. In such cases, the church should elect an Adventist Community Services coordinator (not a director) to coordinate all community services conducted by the local church departments, services, and deacons/deaconesses, which have their individual leaders.

Leaders of Dorcas, Adventist Men, other officially approved local church social ministries organizations, and Adventist Community Services coordinators at the local level participate as members of the Personal Ministries Council under the umbrella of the Personal Ministries Department as stated in this Church Manual.

When community services work is newly organized in a territory, it is recommended to follow the Adventist Community Services model, which involves all church members, in a wide array of community services based on identified needs. For more information go to www.sabbathschoolpersonalministries.org and click on the Adventist Community Services tab.

16. ***Stewardship Ministries Resources*** (see p. 102)—*Steps to Discipleship* (2009). Silver Spring, Md.: Stewardship Ministries, General Conference of Seventh-day Adventists. For further information, contact your local conference, union, or division stewardship ministries department or visit www.adventiststewardship.com.

17. ***Women's Ministries Resources*** (see p. 103)—Leadership certification levels 1-4; resource materials for Day of Prayer, Women's Emphasis Day, and Abuse Prevention Emphasis Day; *Pastor's and Elder's Handbook for Women's Ministries*. For further information, contact your local conference women's ministries director and visit www.adventistwomensministries.org.

18. ***Adventist Youth Ministries Organizational Plan*** (see p. 105)—Detailed information regarding the Adventist Youth Ministries organizational plan is available from the conference youth ministries director. Each church should study its own youth and family profile,

resources, personnel, facilities, and school relationships, developing the best youth ministry in keeping with these factors.

Different terms such as "club," "society," "fellowship," or "action," may be selected, but the name "Adventist Youth" should always be used to clearly identify the organization.

19. **Adventist Youth Ministries Resources** (see p. 109)—Local church officers should first contact their respective conference/mission, union, and division for resources. In addition, the General Conference Youth Ministries Web site also provides support for all levels of youth ministry at www.gcyouthministries.org.

CHAPTER 9 Notes

1. **Sample List of Church Leaders** (see p. 111). The nominating committee selects members to serve as officers in a variety of positions. A small church may have a short list of officers. A large church may have a long list of officers. Here is a list that may be considered:

Elder(s)
Deacon(s)
Deaconess(es)
Clerk
Treasurer and assistant(s)
Interest coordinator
Church board
Church school board
Adventist Community Services leader or Dorcas Society leader
Adventist Community Services secretary-treasurer or Dorcas Society secretary-treasurer
Adventist Youth Ministries leader and associate(s)
Adventist Youth Ministries sponsor
Adventist Youth Ministries secretary-treasurer and assistant
Adventist Youth Ministries music leader
Adventist Youth Ministries pianist or organist
Adventurer Club director
Ambassador Club leader
Bible school coordinator
Children's ministries coordinator
Church chorister or song leader or music coordinator
Church organist or pianist

Communication secretary or communication committee

Education secretary/church school principal or head teacher

Family ministries leader(s)

Health ministries leader

Ministry to People With Disabilities coordinator

Pathfinder Club director and deputy director

Personal ministries leader

Personal ministries secretary

Prayer ministries director

Public campus ministries leader/coordinator

Publishing ministries coordinator

Religious liberty leader

Sabbath School superintendent(s) and assistant(s)

Sabbath School secretary and assistant(s)

Sabbath School division leaders, including leaders for the adult and extension divisions

Sabbath School Investment secretary

Stewardship ministries leader

Vacation Bible School director

Women's ministries leader

Young adults leader

Additional personnel considered necessary

Home and School Association officers (leader and secretary-treasurer): If only one church supports a school, the church nominating committee makes recommendations to the school board, which then makes the appointments. If more than one church supports a school, the school board conducts the whole process. (See pp. 90, 91.)

CHAPTER 10 Notes

1. **Sabbath School** (see pp. 121, 122)—The usual length of time for Sabbath School is one hour and ten minutes. This, however, does not prevent a conference from adopting a longer or shorter period, though it is important to have sufficient time to regularly promote the missionary activities and responsibilities of the world church, along with the mission offering, plus at least thirty minutes for Bible study.

2. **Forms of Service** (see pp. 121-123)—Forms of service vary from country to country and culture to culture. Following are two suggested forms:

Longer Order of Worship

Musical prelude
Announcements
Service participants enter
Doxology
Invocation (prayer)
Scripture reading
Hymn of praise
Prayer
Anthem or special music
Offering
Hymn of consecration
Sermon
Hymn
Benediction
Congregation standing or seated for a few moments of silent prayer
Musical postlude

Shorter Order of Worship

Announcements
Hymn
Prayer
Offering
Hymn or special music
Sermon
Hymn
Benediction
Congregation standing or seated for silent prayer

3. ***Form of Service*** (see p. 122)—As the participants enter and kneel, the congregation should, with bowed heads, implore the presence and blessing of God. A worshipful hush prepares the way for the exercises that follow.

The two main divisions of the worship service are:

a. The congregational response in praise and adoration, expressed in song, prayer, and gifts.

b. The message from the Word of God.

The one leading the worshipers into the presence of God with the pastoral prayer should do so with a sense of awe, realizing its importance. Customarily the person praying kneels facing the congregation, and the congregation, as far as practicable kneeling, in turn faces the individual praying. The prayer should be brief but should include adoration, thanks, and mention of the personal needs of worshippers, as well as of the world field.

The offering is a vital part of the worship hour. While we are counseled to "worship the Lord in the beauty of holiness," we are also exhorted to "bring an offering, and come into His courts" (Ps. 96:9, 8). So the presentation of our gifts to God quite naturally finds its place as a part of the worship service.

Special music or a devotional hymn is appropriate.

Then comes what should be one of the most important parts of the worship hour—the spiritual feeding of the flock of God. Blessed results to the glory of God always follow when a congregation is truly fed and feels that "God has visited His people" (Luke 7:16). The one who brings the message should fully sense the sacredness of this work and should be thoroughly prepared.

The elder collaborates with the church pastor in planning the order of the service. If the church has no regular pastor, the elder is in charge of the service and should either conduct it or arrange for someone to do so. From time to time a meeting for testimony and praise may be conducted, or the time may be given to certain members to relate their experiences in outreach (missionary) work.

4. ***Times of Meetings*** (see p. 122)—In order to strengthen and develop the outreach (missionary) spirit among our members, auxiliary personal ministries meetings might be conducted in one or more of the following ways: a. The ten-minute weekly personal ministries meeting held each Sabbath, usually following the close of the Sabbath School and preceding the preaching service.

b. A midweek meeting combined with the weekly prayer meeting. On this occasion, the first part of the service may be given to a devotional message, followed by a season of prayer, remembering that worship is vital in spiritual growth and preparation for service. The remainder of the time may be devoted to training for lay evangelistic service. Instruction in soul-winning methods is presented, and the members are given opportunity to present and discuss problems they have met in lay evangelism.

Personal ministries meetings should meet at times suited to local conditions. The personal ministries council should carefully plan to make the personal ministries services of the church occasions for spiritual revival and practical training, and see that they are conducted with the same regularity and continuity as other meetings of the church.

5.   ***Foot-Washing*** (see p. 123)—Men and women should be provided separate areas for foot-washing. Where stairs or distance is a problem, special arrangements should be made for those with disabilities. In places where it is socially acceptable and where clothing is such that there would be no immodesty, separate arrangements may be made for husband and wife or parents and baptized children to share with each other in the foot-washing ceremony. To encourage shy or sensitive people who may view the selecting of a foot-washing partner as an embarrassing experience, church leaders should be designated to help such persons find partners.

All should thoroughly wash their hands before returning to participate in the Lord's Supper. Those leading out in the service should do this publicly for hygienic purposes.

6.   ***Bread and Wine*** (see p. 124)—A hymn may be sung during the reassembly of the congregation as the officiating pastors or elders take their places near the bread and wine (unfermented grape juice) and the deacons and deaconesses take their places.

The covering over the bread is removed.

A suitable passage of Scripture may be read, such as 1 Corinthians 11:23, 24; Matthew 26:26; Mark 14:22; or Luke 22:19; or a brief sermon may be given at this point in the service rather than earlier. This can be especially effective if the sermon emphasizes the meaning of the bread and wine so its message is still fresh in the minds of participants as the emblems are being distributed.

Those officiating normally kneel while the blessing is asked on the bread. The congregation may kneel or remain seated.

Usually most of the bread to be served is broken ahead of time, with a small portion left on each plate for the elders and/or pastors to break. (All handling the bread must wash their hands thoroughly before returning for the communion service.) The pastors and elders hand the plates containing the bread to the deacons, who then serve the congregation, though in small congregations the pastor or elders may serve all participants.

During this time there may be a choice of special music, testimonies, a summary of the sermon, selected readings, congregational singing, or meditative music.

Participants should retain their portions of the bread until the officiating pastors or elders have been served. When everyone has been seated, the leader invites all to partake of the bread together. Silent prayers are offered as the bread is eaten.

The pastor then reads a suitable passage, such as 1 Corinthians 11:25, 26; Matthew 26:27-29; Mark 14:23-25; or Luke 22:20. Leaders kneel as the prayer is given over the wine. Again, deacons serve the congregation. Activities such as those suggested during the passing of the bread may be continued at this time. After the officiating pastors or elders have been served, all worshippers partake of the wine together.

An optional method is for the bread to be blessed and broken; then the bread and wine are placed on the same tray and passed to the congregation. The worshipper takes both from the tray at the same time. The bread is eaten, followed by silent prayer. Then after prayer over the wine, it is taken, followed by silent prayer. Where pews or seats are equipped with racks to hold the wine glasses, the collection of glasses is unnecessary until after the service.

7. **Business Meetings** (see p. 128)—Reports may comprise the following activities:

a. A report from the clerk showing the present membership of the church and the number of members received and those transferred to other churches. Note also should be made, giving the number but not necessarily the names of those who were removed from fellowship during the year, as well as those who have died. A brief statement of the decisions of the church board in its meetings may interest members.

b. A report from the personal ministries leader giving a statement of outreach (missionary) activities, including Community Services activities, together with plans for future work. This should be followed by a report from the personal ministries secretary.

c. A report from the treasurer showing the amount of tithe received and sent to the conference, a statement of mission offerings received and forwarded, and a statement showing local church funds received and disbursed.

d. A report from the deacons and deaconesses concerning visits to members, their activities in behalf of the poor, and their other nurturing work.

e. A report from the secretary of the young people's society outlining the activities in outreach (missionary) and other lines by the youth of the church.

f. A report from the Sabbath School secretary giving the membership and other matters pertaining to the Sabbath School.

g. A report from the treasurer about the financial status of the church school, with details as to its needs in equipment and other matters.

h. A report from the principal or teacher of the church school covering such matters as enrollment, the educational progress of the school, baptisms among the schoolchildren, and the results of the children's efforts in denominational endeavors.

i. A report from the Home and School Association leader covering the activities and needs of that organization.

j. A report from the communication secretary covering press, radio, television, and other communication activities involving church and com- munity.

8. ***Other Committees of the Board*** (see p. 132)—Leaders of other board-appointed committees should periodically report. For example, in a large church, the board may appoint a committee for evangelistic planning composed of the heads of the church outreach departments, with an elder as chairperson. This committee will report to the board and will also assume the task of department coordination of outreach programs.

9. ***Adventist Youth Ministries Resources*** (see pp. 133, 134)— Resource materials to help Adventist Youth Ministries leadership are available from the division, union, and conference youth ministries departments. Included in these resource materials is *Youth Ministry Accent*, a quarterly journal published by the General Conference Youth Ministries Department. Available leaflets covering a broad spectrum of topics to help in youth ministry may be secured from the conference youth ministries department and the Adventist Book Center.

CHAPTER 11 Notes

1. ***Stewardship Ministries Resources*** (see p. 137)—*Steps to Discipleship* (2009). Silver Spring, Md.: Stewardship Ministries, General Conference of Seventh-day Adventists. For further information, contact your local conference, union, or division stewardship ministries department or visit www.adventiststewardship.com.

2. **Sample Annual Budget*** (see p. 139).

Church Proposed Operating Budget

Estimated Receipts—

Sabbath School Expense Collections	$ 1,500.00	
Church Fund for the Needy	375.00	
Combined (Church) Budget Giving	27,055.00	
Welfare Fund	300.00	
Total Receipts		$29,230.00

Estimated Expenses—

Repairs and Painting Church Building	$ 2,250.00	
Fuel	2,350.00	
Janitor and Supplies	1,475.00	
Insurance on Building and Furnishings	750.00	
Church Fund for the Needy	1,450.00	
Sabbath School Supplies	1,250.00	
Emergency Expense	2,000.00	
Light	3,220.00	
Water	360.00	
Gas	550.00	
Stationery and Supplies	500.00	
Laundry	75.00	
Church School Subsidy	8,000.00	
Welfare Expense	1,000.00	
Evangelism and Church Planting	4,000.00	
Total Proposed Expenses		$29,230.00
Balance		00,000.00

*Additional columns (such as Last Year's Budget and Last Year's Actual) should be included for comparison, but have been left out of this sample because of space constraints.

Abbreviations

AA	*The Acts of the Apostles*
AH	*The Adventist Home*
CD	*Counsels on Diet and Foods*
CG	*Child Guidance*
CH	*Counsels on Health*
CM	*Colporteur Ministry*
COL	*Christ's Object Lessons*
CSW	*Counsels on Sabbath School Work*
CT	*Counsels to Parents, Teachers, and Students*
CW	*Counsels to Writers and Editors*
DA	*The Desire of Ages*
Ed	*Education*
Ev	*Evangelism*
FLB	*The Faith I Live By*
GC	*The Great Controversy*
GCB	*General Conference Bulletin*
GW	*Gospel Workers*
HP	*In Heavenly Places*
MH	*The Ministry of Healing*
MM	*Medical Ministry*
MYP	*Messages to Young People*
PK	*Prophets and Kings*
PP	*Patriarchs and Prophets*
RH	*Review and Herald*
SC	*Steps to Christ*
T	*Testimonies for the Church*
TM	*Testimonies to Ministers and Gospel Workers*
TMB	*Thoughts From the Mount of Blessing*

General Index

of leader of company, 38
in organizational structure, 26-27
originates with constituency, 113
of parents on Christian lifestyle, 147
of treasurers at any level, 141
Auxiliary organizations
funds, 84
pastor as counselor to, 86
AYM. *See* Adventist Youth Ministries

B

Background check, criminal
for anyone working with minors, 174-175*n*8
children's ministries and, 88
children's SS leaders and, 99
youth ministries' leaders and, 109
Baptism and Commitment, Certificate of, 47-48
Baptism into church membership
about, 43-48
children and, 43
in conference-recognized church, 44
fundamental belief on, 167
inappropriate, 50
instruction/examination before, 44
mode of (by immersion), 44
from other Christian communions, 49
as prerequisite, 43-44
if reconverted, 49-50
of unknown candidates, 48
voting acceptance of, 48

See also Profession of faith; Rebaptism
Baptismal service
assistance with, 48, 81
attire for, 48, 81
covenant document for, 47-48
physical preparations for, 48, 79
public vows for, 45-46
responsibility for, 32, 75
welcome after, 49
Bestiality, 62
Bible correspondence school, 101
Bible evangelism, 101
Bible instructor, 33, 34
Bible school coordinator, 101
Bible study
Christian living and, 143
elders to foster/model, 75
at prayer meeting, 127
SS to promote, 121
See also Sabbath School Bible Study Guide and helps
Birthday/Thank Offering, 100
Board, church
authority limitations of, 54
AYM sponsor from, 108-109
chairpersons of, 32, 74
church business meeting versus, 128
committees of
about, 132, 184*n*8
for baptism examination, 44, 45, 48
for school administration, 90
meetings of, 131
membership/officers of, 130-131
minutes of, 131, 174*n*5
reports to, 132

Q

R

Scripture Index

Index of Sources

TM—Testimonies to Ministers and Gospel Workers

TMB—Thoughts from the Mount of Blessing